Social Media Is About People

Social Media Is About People

Cassandra M. Bailey and Dana M. Schmidt

Leader in applied, concise business books

Social Media Is About People

Cover design by Leo Manning

Interior design by Exeter Premedia Services Private Ltd., Chennai, India

First published in 2022 by
Business Expert Press, LLC
222 East 46th Street, New York, NY 10017
www.businessexpertpress.com

ISBN-13: 978-1-63742-262-5 (paperback)
ISBN-13: 978-1-63742-263-2 (e-book)

Business Expert Press Business Career Development Collection

First edition: 2022

10 9 8 7 6 5 4 3 2 1

Description

Facebook, Instagram, LinkedIn, Pinterest, Twitter, TikTok—the one thing that unites them all is that they are used by people, real human beings. Too often today, marketers are focused on algorithms and analytics instead of simply trying to help their company meaningfully connect with the humans that are going to help them grow.

This book takes a people-first approach to social media that centers on how to best communicate with others using the social media platforms. While each and every social network changes constantly, this underlying approach never will. By ensuring that people are first in all social media strategies, marketers will deliver more value to their companies and the people they serve.

Keywords

marketing; communications; strategy; social media; Facebook; Instagram; LinkedIn; TikTok

Contents

Acknowledgments..ix

Introduction...xi

Chapter 1   A Human-Centered Approach to
             Business Communication 1

Chapter 2   The Six Audiences to Consider and How to
             Prioritize Them..19

Chapter 3   How and Where to Find People......................................41

Chapter 4   Why Listening Matters...49

Chapter 5   How to Talk With People, Not at Them 59

Chapter 6   How People With Influence Can Help 69

Chapter 7   Handling Unhappy People 79

Chapter 8   Building a Human-Centered Social Media Team...........87

Chapter 9   Measuring for Improvement 93

Glossary 95

References...97

Resources 99

About the Authors...101

Index 103

Acknowledgments

Writing this book was easier than we thought it would be because our work every day is so centered in our people-first approach. It is what we do every day, what we speak on at national conferences, and what we instill through our nonprofit, Social Media Day Inc. That said, there are also some very important people who helped make it easy, and we need to thank them.

Jessica Sillers is the main reason we were able to write this book quickly while also running Slice Communications and caring for our families. She was our amazing collaborator and editor, and we hope to one day have the opportunity to work with her again.

Our editor, Vilma Barr, and the team at Business Expert Press, had this crazy idea in 2020 that we could write two books, this one and one on marketing strategy. We were crazy enough to agree, and we are glad we did. We appreciate Vilma's encouragement, guidance, and ambition on our behalf.

Our teams at Slice Communications and Social Media Day Inc. have provided the amazing foundation on which this book was written. Dea Maddox Tuwalski has been our rock, our proofreader, our coach, our translator, and the remover of all barriers. When we doubted whether the book would ever get done, she stepped in and made sure it did. Leo Manning has been our collaborator on everything we have done, including designing the cover of this book and all the graphics within. Marissa Bruette took the time to carefully review these chapters and kept us honest. During the course of writing this book, three individuals joined our Marketing and Book Committee teams. Kija Chronister put a marketing plan in place for the book and helped to manage the editing process. Charlotte Bausch and Mary McCusker came on board and immediately used their copyediting and writing experience to dot every "I" and cross every "T." To Dea, Kija, Charlotte, and Mary—our Book Committee team who drove this book over the finish line—thank you for your many hours of reading, editing, collaboration, and support; you have all be very invaluable throughout this process. Sara McGovern, Rayce Rollins, Andrew Shober, Grace Andrake, Caroline Hromy, Mark Ladley, Aleah Conlin, Matt Smith, Adrian Heredia, Tiffany Coppola, and our whole Slice Fam made sure the business kept running while we worked on the book.

In 2020, we formed a nonprofit organization called Social Media Day Inc. We have been incredibly lucky to work with social media leaders and professionals whose experiences and expertise informed all parts of this book. Our colleagues on the Board of Directors include Andrew Athias, Jason Bannon, Brandi Boatner, Ryan Burchinow, Tom Carusona, Deirdre Childress Hopkins, Danny Gardner, James Gregson, Nicole Heverly, Liz Lenahan, Dea Maddox Tuwalski, Melisa Martinez, Daniel Moise, Rayce Rollins, Lisa Rose, Will Warren Jr., and Tiffany Wilson— as well as our former inaugural year Board colleagues Lola Banjo, Lana Khavinson, Christine Mina, and Jimmy White IV. We are also thankful to all the Social Media Day Inc. members and everyone who speaks at, sponsors, and attends our annual conference. We are constantly inspired and impressed by all the digital marketers and social media professionals in our community.

Our families make all of our hard work worthwhile. We are extremely fortunate to have rock-solid partners in Chris and Jesse. Caia, Cooper, Mia, Alexandra, and Camden, everything is for you and you are everything.

Working in social media is fun. We are very lucky to get to do it every day. We sincerely hope that in reading this book, you will find the fun in it too.

Introduction

Social media is a constantly evolving environment. As this book is being written, the platforms we're covering are actively changing—adapting to new behavioral triggers, trends, and technologies. Aspect ratios will change. Optimal posting cadence will evolve. New best practices for hashtags will emerge. But at their core, what remains the same is that these platforms are social in nature, making them by and for people.

Actual human beings are on the other side of every single post, tweet, or video. These people have wants and needs, dreams and ambitions, stresses and fears. And in some way, those primal drivers are what motivate our own fingers to tap into Facebook, Twitter, LinkedIn, Instagram, Pinterest, TikTok, or any virtual network. We want to know what's happening around us, both at a global level—where news is breaking and culture is being created—and on an intimate one. What are our friends doing? What opportunities are out there for us? How can we entertain ourselves for the next five minutes? Is what we're feeling considered "normal?"

Too often, marketing professionals forget this core element. We become obsessed with "engagement" or how much each click costs. We've been told to "make this go viral" or "sell that product by the end of the month." The social media department has become responsible for responding to customer complaints, engaging employees, and communicating about changes in store hours. If there is not a strong, human-centered approach at the center of all social media efforts, the rest of these things become distractions, taking us further and further from what really matters.

The goal of this book is to help marketers, social media professionals, and business leaders refocus their thinking about this critical communications channel to return to the single most important element: people. The chapters that follow are an opportunity for all of us to break down our current social media strategy and ask why we're investing so much in it and asking so much of it. Because if we hesitate to identify the critical business function social media plays in our organization beyond "everyone else is doing it," we'll quickly find ourselves overextended and underutilizing the most powerful human-to-human communication tool.

In this book, you will learn about the six types of audiences you can interact with on social media and how not only to reach them, but listen to them. Doing this work will elevate the importance of social media within an organization, as it becomes clear it's the primary way businesses should be communicating with the people who matter most to them. Before we do that, let's take a look at the people who use social media in the United States (see Figure I.1).

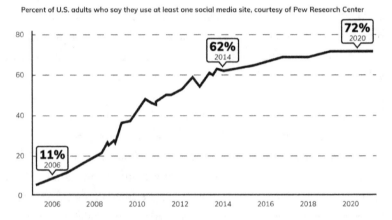

Figure I.1 Social media usage by adults in the US

Pew Research Center 2021

CHAPTER 1

A Human-Centered Approach to Business Communication

Reframing our understanding of social media is essential to begin rebuilding a stronger, human-focused strategy. It is easy to get swept up in the latest tools and trackers, especially when you are adjusting to a platform's new algorithm. Recapturing genuine connections starts with identifying the people we encounter every day, both in real life and on the Web.

Think about your personal network, made up of all the people you have encountered in life. You'll identify some as advocates who stand in your corner and make sure you have what you need. These people feel what you are feeling. They proactively help you create connections, support your projects, and do absolutely whatever they can to help you achieve your goals. Keeping this group informed and engaged makes them want to continue to be part of your success.

Then there are others who can only be found when times are good. They celebrate with you and help you make the most of your opportunities. These cheerleaders want to ride your bandwagon and raise a glass of champagne with you.

Now think of those you turn to when times are tough: the problem-solvers who shoulder your challenges. They'll grab a shovel and help you dig yourself out of trouble at the drop of a hat because of their particular skill set that makes them excel in times of crisis.

You'll also encounter the casual observers. The ones who watch from a distance and will help if needed, as long as it doesn't inconvenience them. These loose acquaintances may have met you at a party or networking event with a big smile on their face, and while they're always happy to cross paths with you, they're not willing to invest in the relationship.

Finally, there are the "undecideds," who float in and out of your orbit over time without establishing themselves in a real category. As of now, neither one of you has decided to investigate or anchor the relationship for whatever reason, but that's not to say "undecided" is a final destination.

What about those people who have decided that they're none of the aforementioned and who are, in fact, actively working against you? While it may be an uncomfortable fact to confront, we all know people who have turned on us. Some may be frustrated by our success and therefore can't be trusted. Other people in this category may be actively undermining our efforts, going so far as to spread rumors and falsehoods in an effort to bruise our reputation. Perhaps they're motivated by a legitimate wrongdoing on our part—an offensive remark we made at a party, a slight (real or perceived) to a family member or friend, or a decision we made that simply wasn't agreeable to all parties involved.

Here's the thing we often forget when we're drafting tweets or designing Instagram grids: These very real people, with all of their varying motivations and degrees of support, exist online behind the handles and usernames connected to your brand and business. They feel these feelings toward you, your organization, and your employees. If in doubt, take a moment to open the social feed of your choice and scroll through the first several posts. Notice the emotion or opinion at the top of your mind when encountering each branded post. Yes, you do have some kind of subjective thought attached to that shoe brand or commercial bank!

In an effort to bring us together, social media has actually created a situation where we are separated from those advocates who are most critical to our success, as well as from warning signs from people who could harm our work or prevent us from achieving our goals. With our audiences sitting on the other end of an Internet connection, we lose the intimacy that occurs by sharing a physical space, whether it's a boardroom or a brick-and-mortar shop. As platforms such as Twitter, Instagram, and Snapchat launched or expanded between 2010 and 2013, many companies did not follow their communities into these spaces and lost important chances to communicate with people.

Instead, we have been focused on informal communication and inhuman communication locked into a digital format. We spend more time thinking about algorithms and vanity "engagements" than actual conversations and questions. We're focused on what our web analytics point to instead of what people are sharing about their feelings and experiences. We are taking humanity out of our marketing in our business communications.

We cannot tell you how many times we have spoken with marketers today who tell us about their click-through rate. They talk about how many people follow them on Facebook or how many views their video just earned. What they do not talk about, and frankly, what they do not know, is who is doing the clicking, following, and viewing. They don't know how to actually have conversations with real human beings. They are so focused on crafting a post to use "optimized" language with the right hashtags that they don't pause to consider how two human beings would have this conversation in real life, face to face.

Most new marketers entering the field spend their entire college careers learning the technical aspect of the industry. Focusing only on the data-driven side of marketing weakens our ability to actually talk with people. Writing is challenging, and persuasive writing, the style that convinces someone to take action, takes immense skill and practice. How do you incorporate the nuance of compelling language into social posts in a way that sounds natural? How do you inspire through words and visuals?

While there is great value in making data-driven decisions and relying on strategic tests to determine effectiveness, we can't lose our gut sense in the thick of it all. Making it to the top of the Instagram feed isn't the end-all, be-all goal. We need to listen to our gut and trust our human intuition a bit more in order to be truly impactful in the long term. Showing up in the feed is only half the battle; how our messages are received and internalized matters deeply to the success of a company.

We have been able to hire dozens of young marketers over the years at our agency. In our discussions about growth opportunities, many of them have admitted to struggling with telephone conversations with clients. They hesitate to ask the probing questions. They don't quite know how to listen between the lines. They're often in such a hurry to get to work that they're reluctant to slow the pace of the call down so they can really identify the client's unspoken needs or concerns. When we're so focused on crossing the next thing off our list, like scheduling one more post or drafting one more e-mail, we're missing the opportunity to have that meaningful conversation with the client. These real-time connections are a crucial point in setting ourselves up for success. How can we be present and purposeful in our audience-facing communication if we're not present and purposeful on these calls?

There is a lot of work to be done in teaching people how to have productive conversations with others. Most of the time, this inability to communicate on the phone and have back-and-forth discussions is rooted in deep insecurity. When we lack confidence in ourselves, we can't comprehend how our work—how our distinct voice—will contribute to the overall success of the business. This insecurity leads to a place where we are just rushing to a fictional finish line, getting things done without really understanding *why* they need to be done and what it is going to mean for the business. This action orientation takes our focus away from doing work that is meaningful.

As a young public relations (PR) professional, Cass has had the opportunity to sit in on a number of media training sessions with clients and executives. A conversation with reporters is unlike any other conversation you will ever have in your life. That's because when we are talking with reporters, our job isn't to answer questions. This goes against everything we learn in life. But when we are speaking with a reporter, in our role as a spokesperson, our job is actually to deliver a message that best represents our company—to speak to the audience of that reporter's story. We need to use that reporter's original question as a vehicle to communicate our most important messages as part of our response, to make sure that people know what we need them to know and to position ourselves effectively. Our response is engineered to achieve a business goal.

Cass was taught to use a media training exercise in which the spokesperson imagines themselves in a stadium. When speaking to a reporter, that spokesperson is looking beyond the single individual in front of them and instead to the 70,000 fans filling the stands. Thousands of the most important people who can make or break your business: clients, customers, employees, investors, donors, suppliers, partners, detractors, competitors, legislators, and others. The people filling the stadium are the ones that matter and yet, when we send a tweet or produce a video for Facebook, we often do not visualize the stadium like we teach in media training. In fact, we rarely pause to imagine a single fan, waving a figurative foam finger for us. Building in that pause to visualize the stadium is the big goal of this book, and it should be the big goal of all of your business communications moving forward.

Take a second to think about the most important conversation you have ever had in your business. Really take the time to think about it deeply, reliving as much of it as you can. You might even want to grab a pencil and paper, if you're the type to think with your hands, and jot down what jumps out in response to these questions:

- With whom did you have this conversation?
- What was the goal of the discussion?
- Where did it take place?
- How long did the conversation last?
- Did it evolve into a series of smaller conversations with other stakeholders?
- What words or phrases stick in your mind from that conversation and did they come from you or the other person?
- What gestures or analogies did you use?
- Did you tell a story?
- Did you show visuals?
- Did you include data?

Now try to remember: What was the outcome? Did you achieve what you set out to achieve in its entirety? How did you feel when it was over— and did all parties involved agree that it was in fact over?

If you can distill the most important lessons you learned from this conversation, your next step is to assess where else you can apply those lessons in your business. At the very least, you should be able to use these questions to create a detailed framework that can give you insights into your conversational style.

Now think about the most ineffective conversation you have ever had in your business. One that felt like a waste of time and resources or left you frustrated. Expand on that definition:

- What made the conversation "ineffective" for you?
- Were you unclear in your communication, or did you have the sense that the other person wasn't understanding you well, even if you thought you were being clear?
- Were you having the conversation with the wrong person?
- Were you having the conversation at the wrong time?
- Was the conversation in the wrong forum?
- Were there others in the room who worked against you?
- Were you unprepared or lacking the proper context and education on the issue at hand?
- Did you take the time to really listen to all parties involved to understand what they wanted or needed, or were you rushed?
- Conversely, did the conversation leave you feeling unheard?

Everything we post on social media can, and should, be an opportunity for a new conversation. It should open the lines of communication. It should support all parts of the business.

One way we encourage social media managers to think about their social and digital communications as human-centered is to assign job descriptions to each social platform and the company website. That way, we can understand the critical role that our social media plays within our company and how it supports our overall growth. We assign each social channel goals and expectations, and hold it accountable for helping us achieve success.

Facebook: The Awareness and Engagement "Neighbor"

If each social media channel needs its own job description, let's begin with a heavy hitter: Facebook. Most American adults are on Facebook daily and they check it multiple times a day. Think about how Facebook is most commonly used. We log in to connect with friends and stay in the loop on major life announcements such as growing families and big moves. We sign on to discover and check the news. To find out what is happening in our neighborhood. To be entertained in between meetings. To research new products or brands. To look for new job opportunities. To ask for advice.

So, what is Facebook's role in your company? Facebook is the primary business-to-person channel because of its advanced targeting capabilities and expansive communities. Facebook really leads the industry in terms of giving marketers the tools to build a niche audience, so on a granular level, you can reach a very unique customer with a solution to their problem. The platform has also created groups that act as niche enclaves for people to gather over shared interests and concerns. Unlike a platform like LinkedIn, where users tend to be in a professional mindset while scrolling, Facebook audiences are on the platform for the personal side of things: joining groups and conversations on neighborhood events, parenting advice, and healthy lifestyle tips, to name a few. If you are trying to demonstrate how your brand fits into existing routines and solves common stresses, this is a good place to be—particularly if you're selling consumer products or services. If you rely on community support and need on-the-ground advocacy, Facebook can help. If you are trying to provide people with new opportunities related to their career, some of that work can be accomplished here—although we wouldn't want to create too much overlap with our LinkedIn job description.

Facebook, for most companies, can be an impressive powerhouse for generating awareness and meaningful engagement with the general adult population, especially if your strategy involves paid targeting. So include that specific expectation in a job description. What is it responsible for? Three possible "essential job functions" for Facebook could include:

- Generate top-of-funnel awareness with new audiences.
- Grow loyal connections and celebrate existing centers of influence and advocates who follow you.
- Deepen engagement with audiences who have indicated they are interested in learning more about your brand, perhaps through retargeting website visitors.

Ask yourself: How will you know if Facebook is doing its job? You can track top-of-funnel awareness through a measurable increase in reach. If loyal connections and advocates are a top goal, track how often you're being introduced to new people on this channel through an increase in followers. Evaluate engagement by checking how often you start conversations with new folks. Are you noticing an increase in Facebook-driven traffic back to your website or Facebook-driven purchases? This will tell you if you're capturing visitors' attention and nudging them toward the next stage of the funnel.

Our agency operates as business-to-business (B2B): Our services support other companies in developing their social media, PR, and e-mail marketing strategies. One of our biggest client opportunities came through Facebook. A colleague at the time was connected with someone else who knew about an opportunity to work with a company that was entering the Philadelphia market. That friend, a contact from college, introduced us to the company, which was tasked with hiring a Philadelphia regional agency. We were selected as one of three agencies to go in and pitch, and we won. Because of Facebook. Even though its job was not to develop new business for us—its job was to keep us connected to people who care about us and want to see us succeed. So, you could say Facebook got a promotion.

Today, we frequently use Facebook as a recruiter. It's been incredibly effective in helping us find new employees. We also use it to stay top-of-mind and connected with all the people who really care about us and our personalized content. We share information on Facebook in a way that is casual and conversational; it's fun with an educational slant. The friendly, engaging tone that we use on this channel positions us as likeable and relatable. We don't take ourselves too seriously.

Facebook can keep its job if it continues to earn us awareness, and we measure that by earning impressions with the right audiences. We are constantly tracking reach and studying the demographics and behaviors of our followers behind the numbers. We're not evaluating Facebook's success by looking at leads generated here—and the reason is because we don't expect conversions to happen on this platform. As a B2B company, we know our audience isn't necessarily in the "purchasing mindset" on Facebook. We want to be seen here and remembered as a valuable resource, but asking Facebook to do too much is like assigning sales, IT, and HR responsibilities to the same employee.

Business-to-consumer (B2C) companies are very different. Some can use Facebook to sell their products, if done appropriately. But from our experience, a common mistake is to put the cart before the horse and focus on conversion through Facebook before awareness or engagement. When you think about Facebook's job, give it reasonable expectations and regularly evaluate it, just as you would a valued employee.

LinkedIn: Recruiting, Partnerships, and B2B Promotion

LinkedIn is primarily a B2B channel. One of its top functions is to share news and accomplishments happening within the company. When a company has an important announcement to share, it happens here. Businesses go to LinkedIn to promote awards they've won or major honors they've received. We see employers highlighting their employees' speaking engagements and blog posts–even just spotlighting their hobbies and personal lives that give a peek into company culture.

Because LinkedIn users create a profile that shows their professional side, rather than their personal life, this platform is where many sales people and recruiters make their living. People often solidify a new contact they met at a conference or webinar by sending a connection request on LinkedIn. It's where sales teams prospect new business and identify potential opportunities. And as COVID-19 created a major shift in how we all interact with one another, LinkedIn replaced in-person networking as a digital reception of sorts.

Many B2C companies use LinkedIn primarily for recruiting and hiring. But that is not the only job it can handle. It can create strategic partnerships and joint venture collaborations. It's a place to stay connected with suppliers and others who are critical to the business' success. Cass personally has a goal—and has for many years, even prepandemic—of making seven new connections every week. This is how she keeps her network healthy and maintained—by nurturing it on a home like LinkedIn. It's also often the easiest way to help people, by bridging opportunities and introducing new relationships. And helping people has always been one of the core foundations of the business that we run.

LinkedIn's job description at our company is to earn us meaningful connections through thought leadership. We use LinkedIn to share new ideas and new insights with others and pose questions that make people rethink their processes. It's where we promote business-focused events that we host, seeing as those are prime networking opportunities. LinkedIn is where we celebrate wins and amplify the good work we're accomplishing with clients. We need the human beings behind the professional headshots and polished resumes to find value in following us, ideally picturing us as a potential partner.

Twitter: Real-Time, Fast-Paced Customer Service, and Promotion

Twitter is our primary listening channel and our primary "in real-life" channel. Unlike Facebook, where someone's feed may be made up mostly of personal and local connections, Twitter is often a go-to social platform to connect to a broader community of like-minded folks who share a common culture or interest. People show up to keep a finger on the pulse of the daily discourse and get news information. Most people who are on Twitter actually never tweet. On more than one occasion, when we've asked a client how they use Twitter, they've described themselves as "lurkers." They are just there to understand what is happening. It becomes their curated news feed. They choose what is in their feed and who they get information from. So think about this as you are designing a Twitter strategy.

Twitter's job description in your business could be to make sure that you are staying top-of-mind with people and creating new brand awareness. This is the right platform for people who are looking for information that you have an opinion or new point of view about. Twitter is also highly discoverable. If you are trying to introduce a new product or service, Twitter could be a great place to do that as long as you can tap into conversations where people are talking about what it is that you have to offer. Twitter is also able to support your company in terms of interacting with thought leaders. If there are people who have a large following or a lot of influence on Twitter because their tweets have a wide reach, there could be a benefit to getting their attention.

You may also want to think about Twitter in terms of live event support. As we mentioned, it's our primary "in real-life" channel. That means when people are actually out and about doing fun and interesting things, they are talking about it on Twitter. You'll see conferences and events encouraging people to find each other on Twitter to share real-time impressions and generate discussion about what's happening. Twitter is primarily an open platform. You can respond to, and interact with, anybody. So this can be a live event hub for you to open up conversations with new audiences and get an up-to-the-minute check on how your audience is responding without being in five places at once. If your goal is finding people in the same geographic areas as you, attending the same event, supporting causes you support, or sharing new opinions that tie closely in with your company's core values, Twitter is a great place to do that.

Twitter can also be a great place to get quick feedback and interaction outside of special events. That is why some companies have determined that customer service is the primary job description of Twitter, with some promotional tweets mixed in for their current customers. If you do not have a customer service plan for Twitter, it may be the first thing that you need to create in terms of your overall social media strategy. Twitter is a fast-paced platform, so customer conversations with in-real-time responses tend to do best. Look at how often you are mentioned on Twitter and read up so you understand which people are looking for you on that platform and what they need. This way, you can figure out a strategy that fits with how people are already prepared to engage with you.

Finally, Twitter is a great place to be if one of your goals is market research. You can do a lot of listening there. Hear what people are saying about your brand without interacting with them. Hear what they are saying about your competitors. Hear what your competitors are saying. It might be worth your while to be one of those users who's on Twitter, but rarely tweets, especially if you don't have the bandwidth right now to hit quick, reliable response times with customers. Twitter's job at your company could be to do that research and do that listening so you're caught up and prepared when the right opportunity arises to enter the conversation. So don't dismiss Twitter as just a place where people go to outdo each other with inside jokes or spend a bathroom break scrolling (although plenty of that happens, too). Use it as a place of meaningful conversations and interactions, and do some real listening.

Instagram: Emotional, Visual Connection

Instagram is our primary visual channel. It's where people go to post photos and videos of what they are doing in order to build the brand of who they are. But it's also a huge shopping platform. Because Instagram is so aspirational, it's a great place to find people who are looking for new shoes, skin products, restaurants, or basically any product or experience that fits the visual inspiration they're hoping to bring into their own life. If you are trying to sell a consumer product, focus on how it enhances your audience's lifestyle, from "date night" experiences, to travel destinations, to nutritional plans.

Companies that are already geared toward highly visual luxury products, services, and experiences likely won't have trouble developing the job description for Instagram. But what about companies with something less obviously photogenic to offer? Instagram can still play an active role in your social media strategy, if you assign it the right job.

We're seeing a business evolution of companies using Instagram in order to recruit new employees. What that looks like is using Instagram as a tool to present your office, showcase your employees (or your employees' dogs!), and feature anything else that makes your firm or your company more likable. Especially for younger audiences, the visual matters. A picture really is worth a thousand words. Instagram creates an atmosphere and connects to emotions in a way that other social platforms don't, because Instagram is intended to be all about feelings and visuals. Someone looking at your profile can get an immediate, emotion-based impression of your company based on the cues in your visual style.

As you are thinking about Instagram's job description within your company, these are some signs this channel has a role to play for you:

- If you have big recruiting goals.
- If you are trying to connect with Millennial and
  Gen Z audiences.
- If you are trying to create brand awareness for something new.

According to Hootsuite, about 90 percent of people on Instagram follow at least one business (Newberry 2021). As you put together your

Instagram profile and advertising plan, you can do a lot of very detailed targeting and find the right people who actually care about the value that you have to offer because it connects with what they're looking for in that moment. Since Facebook owns Instagram, all of the advanced tools available to marketers on Facebook carry over here, allowing you to build incredibly niche audiences again.

Instagram is also one of the most rapidly evolving channels, as it tends to learn from emerging channels and absorb their best features. If your company is curious about Snapchat, test Instagram Stories first—a similar ephemeral photo and video feature that Instagram built in response to Snapchat's success. As people tend to gravitate more toward this visually rich, behind-the-scenes way of communicating their brand to their networks, you too, as a marketer, can express your company's messages in a similar way so that it resonates with your audience.

If you've been considering dipping a toe in TikTok, try Instagram's Reels, their response to TikTok's success. The videos tend to be more produced than Instagram Stories and function to entertain communities rather than inform on personal brands. If your brand has a lighthearted approach to voice and tone, Reels could be a fun playground to explore.

While it's true for all social media channels, it's especially important for Instagram since there are several options for publishing content: meet your audience where they are, and make sure that comes across in its job description.

Pinterest: The Lifestyle Search Engine

Pinterest is primarily a lifestyle channel. People go there to find inspiration to enhance the way that they live. They look for new ways to decorate their homes, throw parties, celebrate a wedding, explore new recipes, find exercise ideas, and plan the perfect picnic. Most of the lifestyle activities that are most popular on Pinterest are primarily driven by women, and we know that most of the audience on Pinterest is women (Statista Research Department 2021).

Pinterest also has the highest average user household income of any of the social media channels. This means that people browsing Pinterest are realistically looking for things to spend money on. They have expendable income, and whether they want to buy things or engage in new travel experiences—they are basically looking for ways to spend money. For this reason, if you have products, services, expertise, or insight on how to make this group of mostly affluent, mostly female users spend their money better, Pinterest is the place for you.

Pinterest is a social media platform, but its job description at your company should look more like your goals for a search engine than a social media site such as Facebook. While you can find a back-and-forth in terms of comments or likes between people on Pinterest, the most important thing to remember is that people on Pinterest often click through to visit the page the image connects to. For that reason, Pinterest is used to drive a tremendous amount of traffic—or it could be. If your business is just posting photos without creating links where people can buy what they're viewing, sign up for a newsletter, or register for a demo, then you have lost the opportunity that Pinterest provides.

Pinterest, like Twitter and Instagram, is also highly discoverable. People often search for posts that match their interests, and a high percentage of users are interested in trying new things, compared to people on other social media sites. That means that if you have a presence on Pinterest because you are looking for that target demographic, making a Pinterest page can increase your natural search engine optimization. Depending on your industry, you may be able to achieve a high click-through rate, even from people who are new to your business. So creating brand awareness is certainly a way to use Pinterest and something that you can put in its job description. But you can also assign it the task of driving traffic to your website and potentially driving sales directly.

YouTube: Entertainment, Education, and Searchability

YouTube is the world's second-largest search engine. Only Google tops it—and happens to own it. That means that YouTube is both a social network and a library of content, promoting your product, service, and business to people who are searching.

The easiest job description to assign YouTube is for it to be a centralized platform for all of your video content. The misstep to avoid is undermining your efforts on other social media channels. Facebook, LinkedIn, and Twitter are putting energy into increasing views and keeping people on their platform. We used to post links from YouTube onto Facebook, LinkedIn, and Twitter, but that behavior is being discouraged by those platforms right now. You'll get better results from a native video uploaded directly to those channels instead of redirecting them to YouTube. A good strategy is to clip a longer YouTube video for the optimal time for the alternate platform it's served on (i.e., 30 seconds for Facebook) and then invite your audience to view the entire video on YouTube. YouTube still plays a valuable role as a place where people will spend a tremendous amount of time.

Many young people will say that YouTube is their primary form of entertainment today. It is also a place where people go to learn things. For that reason, if your business is focused on education, sharing new ideas, or demonstrating new products, then YouTube might be the place for you. In this example, YouTube's job description is to increase your reach and build your reputation as a thought leader by positioning your business as an authority when people search for answers or solutions to a problem you solve. In this scenario, when creating content for YouTube, start by identifying what questions your audience is asking. Your YouTube videos should be built around answering them.

YouTube is also a great place to look for people who could potentially become your advocates, the people we discussed at the beginning of this chapter who provide the strongest connection and support. People invest tremendous resources in becoming YouTube influencers, both in terms of their time and money. Doing market research on people on their way to becoming influencers can help you discover advocates for you. The other market research "job" YouTube has at your business is researching your audience and competitors. You want to understand what your audience is consuming on this platform and what your competitors are doing to capture their attention.

As with every social platform, you need to adapt your measure of success to fit the role you want this channel to perform for you. Metrics like the number of views may vary in importance based on whether you're using YouTube as a tool to expand brand awareness, educate, or cultivate relationships and partnerships with influencer advocates.

TikTok: The Star of the Moment

Whether TikTok will stand the test of time is still to be determined. As of January 2022, TikTok had over one billion monthly active users and

167 million TikTok videos watched in an "Internet minute" each day (Geyser 2022). That's too big of a market to ignore—if they're the right audience for your business and if this platform lasts. If you're reading this book years after we sat down to write it, you might be laughing at our uncertainty about this relatively new platform. You may also be scratching your head, wondering, "What is TikTok?"

The big benefit of TikTok is that it is addictive. Its algorithm is designed to be the most advanced of its type to serve up content—in this case, specifically video content—that keeps your attention on the app. People talk about going down the rabbit hole because TikTok is incredibly good at serving you new videos based on something else that you liked, watched to completion, or shared with friends. If your content on TikTok is tied to something that is popular or trending, like a song or audio clip, you have a chance to show up organically in front of that audience. That said, your brand and content needs to be highly entertaining, funny, a little tongue-in-cheek, and very much of the moment in order to perform well on TikTok. Your audience also needs to fit the young, trendy, fun-seeking crowd, or you'll struggle to achieve meaningful results on TikTok.

TikTok truly is about people, almost more than any other social media channel. By that we mean, in order for your content to really excel in this space, you need to have a person hosting your video. There needs to be a face on screen—someone to tell your story and connect with the audience on a human level. While some brands have had success without this component, they are few and far between. To that end, if TikTok is something you think your brand should pursue, someone on your marketing team should have TikTok in *their* job description.

The bottom line is that a human-centered approach to social media marketing means that you need to think about the people who use the platforms, not just the platforms themselves. Thinking of the platforms as people and giving them job descriptions will put you on the right track (see Exercise 1.1).

Social Media's Job Description

Channel Name:

Who Are We Trying to Reach?
- ☐ Customers / Clients
- ☐ Employees
- ☐ Centers of Influencer

- ☐ Partners / Suppliers
- ☐ Investors / Donors
- ☐ Competitors

What is the channel's responsibility?

What content do you need for this channel?

Written

Visual

Video

Audio

Experiential

What does success look like?

What metrics are we tracking?

Exercise 1.1 Social media's job description

CHAPTER 2

The Six Audiences to Consider and How to Prioritize Them

Too often, business leaders tell us that anyone can be their customer. While technically true for some, that approach to marketing is doomed to fail. Marketing to everyone means marketing to no one. There are very few situations in the history of humankind where a product or service can solve a problem every single human has. The COVID-19 pandemic in 2020 could be one example, and companies that developed effective vaccines benefited. Even in this case, though, with something as theoretically universal as a vaccine for a deadly disease, we've seen controversy over getting the shot. If people self-select out of being the "target customer" for a solution to a highly contagious virus, that's a strong signal to any company to focus our marketing efforts on the people who want to hear what we have to say.

Before we dive into the six potential audiences your business may want to target, let's revisit what we know about people. There are two ways to categorize them: demographics and psychographics.

Most marketing defines people by their demographics, which are characteristics often associated with objectively observable facts. Some examples of demographics include:

- Age
- Gender
- Race
- Income
- Education
- Location

- Religion
- Marital status
- Job title
- Number of children
- Pet ownership

These things can be helpful in determining what we know about our most promising audiences in order to easily locate others like them. However, defining people just based on their demographics misses their humanity. It also ignores the most powerful way we can connect with each other: through emotions.

Psychographics is the study of people based on subjective qualities such as their feelings, dreams, opinions, fears, beliefs, and attitudes. Understanding these help us connect with our audiences much more fully. It significantly increases the speed with which we can get their attention because we can connect with something within them that is true and real. It helps us keep their attention because they feel heard, seen, and understood by communication that is meant for them and people who believe the same things they do. Examples of psychographics include:

- Values
- Fears
- Influences
- Concerns
- Dreams
- Information sources
- Brand loyalties
- Insecurities
- Stresses
- Joys

Quite often, we will find similarities in our best customers across all these different psychological characteristics. They value helping others or dream about owning their own businesses or struggle with addiction or really want the next promotion. Regardless of who your most important audience is, it is critical that you know about their psycho-graphics and demographics. Anything short of that will mean that your marketing strategy is largely uninformed, which will cause a real prob-lem when it comes to developing messaging and content that engages your audience effectively.

Often, marketing communications people focus their energy entirely on one group: customers and clients. This has historically been the most important audience. But as business has become more complex, there are other people that can help or hurt. Getting specific about which audience is the intended recipient of each message will exponentially increase the effectiveness of your marketing.

There are three important caveats. First, marketing to one audience doesn't mean that you will offend another. You can choose messages, cam-paigns, and images that create an emotional connection with one group and barely register with another. That's okay. It's also okay if one group gives you a lot of engaged attention based on a campaign while you just get a little attention from another. That is the reality of making choices. As the famous strategist Michael Porter says, "Strategy is about making choices along *many* dimensions, not just *one*. No single prescription about which choices to make is valid for every company in every indus-try" (Magretta 2011, 32). In other words, strategy is about trade-offs; it's about deliberately choosing to be different.

The next important caveat about prioritizing one audience is that it doesn't mean you have to be committed to that audience for the rest of history. Your audience is going to change over time. For instance, your company might not have the capacity to service all the demand in the market. It would make sense to change the focus from custom-ers to potential employees for a time. The marketing plan might focus on promoting the best employees in order to get more of them. Would promoting your employees' stories and experiences offend your custom-ers? Of course not! People love to work with companies that value their employees and showcase them.

The third important caveat when identifying and prioritizing audi-ences is that you need to focus on those you want, not those you happen to have. We cannot express to you how many times we have been asked this question while helping companies define their target audiences. Some have a very hard time acknowledging that the people whose attention they have today are not the same people whose attention they are going to need in the future. It becomes easily apparent when they are defining the demographics and psychographics of an audience, and they start complaining. No one complains about their ideal audience. No one. If you find yourself or someone else talking this way, stop the conversation and refocus it on what you want. If the complaining continues, chances are that the person doing the complaining is not prepared to assist in the company's future growth.

Creating alignment within your organization in terms of developing a clear marketing plan almost always comes down to agreeing on the audience. Discuss all six potential options during those conversations to help identify underlying issues, concerns, and confusion. When you feel comfortable identifying the people and organizations that belong to each of the following groups, you're much more prepared to reach the right audience, at the right time, with a message that speaks to their unique experience.

Customers and Clients

Most marketing is focused on customers and clients. It pretty much always has been, and that makes sense because marketing mostly supports sales. What's surprising given this emphasis is that most marketers spend little or no time talking with customers and clients. We've never understood why customer service and marketing are separate functions within a business. The most important information marketers need to develop strategy includes:

- What do customers care about?
- What problem are we solving for them?
- What do we do well?
- What do they wish we could do better?
- What do they say when they complain?
- What confuses them about what we do that we can make easier to understand?

All of this psychographic information is often held by customer service representatives or account managers. Marketers rarely get to see it, and when they do, it is usually in a very general report and only in companies large enough to have people dedicated to market research.

The good news is that social media has made it significantly easier to understand customers because so many of them complain online. Some large companies now have entire teams dedicated to customer service through Twitter. If you're handling your organization's social media channels, you probably have a strong sense of common customer complaints, what they need and care about, and what works and what does not when talking with them. The downside is that those jobs are often stressful and exhausting, particularly since people are willing to be angrier and more aggressive behind their computer screens. You may spend a lot of time handling daily concerns and questions, but people working in social media don't always have the bandwidth or even the authority to make high-level marketing changes themselves. As a result, many people who work in those jobs burn out quickly.

Similarly, there are often big gaps between sales, marketing, and social media teams. Salespeople are notoriously bad at sharing information, leads, and success stories outside of "hitting their numbers." This doesn't need to be the case. We know a marketing professional who made it her job to get to know a handful of the salespeople personally. She took them to lunch, hung out with them over coffee, and was even invited to listen in on their sales conversations with prospective customers. This made her the most informed person on her team, and she was able to develop some really innovative campaigns just by being the best listener. Likewise, we know a business development person who realized the power of marketing to help him sell. He would send the marketing department doughnuts, comment on their LinkedIn posts for the company, and volunteer to help at trade shows. He had no trouble ensuring that he had marketing materials that spoke to his segment of the customer base.

Marketers and those responsible for developing marketing and social strategy for customers really must focus on finding good stories from the best audiences. These stories will help with all the types of attention necessary to move people from awareness to advocacy.

All marketing to clients and customers is about meeting them where they are. For a student loan company trying to get students to take or refinance loans, that opportunity was March Madness. For certain students at basketball-obsessed universities, most of which have large populations, there is nothing more exciting and no better time to express school pride. The company wanted to generate as much awareness as possible, with the secondary goal of collecting e-mail addresses.

In order to achieve the company's goals, our team knew we had to offer something with high perceived value. Utilizing the company's website, we created a landing page with an entry form where students submitted pictures of the "main street" on their college campus and their contact information in order to enter. We directed people back to the page through a series of social media posts, which included a targeted paid campaign. Over the course of six rounds, different schools went head-to-head March Madness style. People could vote once per day for the school of their choice in each matchup. Every time a school advanced, the cumulative prize increased. People whose photo won the most votes in the round advanced and received scholarships ranging from one hundred dollars to the grand prize of $2,150.00. The champion was also able to donate one thousand dollars to the charity of their choice.

The campaign was incredibly successful. The day it launched, there were 28,000 visits to the website, the highest volume for a single day in the company's history. The website almost crashed. Overall, the campaign encouraged thousands of people to participate, generating over 1,500 e-mail addresses of college students. The company also benefited from almost half a million social media impressions from their target audience of college students.

Employees

In recent conversations, we have had with CEOs and leadership team members, their focus has shifted away from the customer audience being the priority. Many recognize that the growth they want to achieve is only possible if they have the right employees. Lacking enough employees, or the right employees, is the single biggest thing holding them back. In many cases, these companies are turning away work from customers because they do not have the people they need to do it. This is particularly true in distribution, e-commerce, essential retail, technology, manufacturing, insurance, and professional services.

As a result, these CEOs and leaders are shifting their focus to employees. They must, for the first time in many cases, focus on getting attention for their company as an employer—not just as a product or service provider.

Creating an employer brand is not enough, though. You can absolutely be the employer of choice in your industry or geography, but if no one knows it, you will never achieve your goals. Before you continue reading, know this: Building and promoting an external brand is not something that can be done alone. There may be some false starts and some barriers along the way. But there is a double benefit: People will want to work for you. And your customers will likely feel great about choosing a company that cares about its people.

Traditionally, the human resources (HR) department is responsible for finding these new employees and helping them acclimate into the company. But there is a clear divide between HR and marketing, and that silo is what needs to be destroyed in order to recruit well to fill the talent gap.

Before we go any further on the employee audience or you decide it's your priority, we must share an important warning. Successful employer branding requires that a strong, positive culture is already in place. If you are struggling with culture, please contact an HR consultant who specializes in that work. Marketing falsely to potential employees or creating a false perception of your workplace will backfire. Employees who take jobs will leave. Worse, they will let anyone who listens know about their experience with your company.

Because most companies have never prioritized their employees as a marketing audience before, they need to understand how their company culture is perceived, where their strengths are, and what great stories they can tell. There are nine tools that can determine how different groups see your employer brand:

- **Employee Survey**—We all know what this is. Make sure whatever you're using includes questions about how they describe the culture and whether they think it is an employer of choice. Also ask for specific examples of experiences they've had that demonstrate the culture. This will let you know if they are sharing genuine feedback, and these stories can become great content in the future.

- **Applicant Survey**—This is one of the most overlooked sources of information. People apply for jobs because they want to improve their current situation. Chances are, you already have a database of them with their e-mail addresses, the position(s) for which they applied, and their geography. Ask them a few questions either during the screening process or after about why they applied to work with you, what they think your culture is, and how they learned about the company. Sure, most of this will be complimentary since they want to work for you, but you will learn pretty quickly if there is a common perception that is not aligned with the image you want to convey.

- **Mission, Vision, and Values Worksheet**—This is not about whether your company has a written mission, vision, and values. You should already have those in place. Instead, you need to be clear about HOW you're delivering on those statements. What are the stories? How do you live these values? Who are the people who are the best examples of them? How well are your words becoming actions?

- **Online Reputation Audit**—Most people find open positions online. All people research companies online. So what does your online presence say about you as an employer? What copy, images, and videos are on your "About" and hiring website pages? What does your LinkedIn company page look like? What about the personal LinkedIn pages of your hiring and management team members? What about your other social channels? What about third-party websites? Have current or former employees written reviews on Glassdoor, Google, or Facebook that support or degrade your business? Has anyone else written about you as an employer? You need to know these answers to know how you are being perceived.

- **Awards and Recognition**—If you've won awards, what are they for and who gave them to you? More importantly, what

other awards do you want to get in the future? Doing this
work will help you realize how you want to be positioned in
the market and who will give you credibility. Look at other
companies who have received those awards to get some
insight into who your competitors for talent are.

- **Champion Readiness Review**—Champions are your current
  employees who can become your ambassadors. We're going
  to talk about them more in the "Building the Team" section.
  But first things first: You need to identify them. Who are the
  people you want to showcase so you can attract more employees like them? Select a group of people diverse in age, background, and experience so that you can showcase the variety
  of people who will work well in your company. Also spend a
  little time thinking and talking about how ready this group
  of people is. Is there a person who is already a great writer?
  Already really good on video? Already a LinkedIn rock star?
  Already referring people to work at the company? These will
  be important factors as you think about training and deploy-
  ing them to external audiences.

- **Diversity and Inclusion Commitment**—If you care about
  having a diverse workforce (however you define it), you need
  to carefully evaluate how effectively you are delivering on this
  promise. Do you have internal or external programs to attract
  and welcome employees who are different from your current
  staff? Are these programs well-resourced and effective? Or are
  they just lip service and everyone knows it? Where are the
  opportunities to improve?

- **Job Description Audit**—Most applicants will read a job
  description before applying. But most of them are bland and
  boring—sure, they may list the company values and some of
  the benefits, but they rarely communicate anything about the
  feeling of working there. Take a look at your job descriptions.
  What is the process by which they are written? What words
  are used effectively? What words and phrases are missing? If
  a potential employee only read this, what would that person
  feel about the company?

- **Content Review**—All companies today produce content.
  There are five types: written, visual, audio, video, and experiential. What does your content communicate? Is it aggressive?
  Generic? Warm? Exclusive? Technical? Does it help or hurt
  how you want to be perceived as an employer?

After you've done all this work, it's time to get the leadership, HR, and
marketing teams together to review them. From there, there needs to be
agreement on the types of employees you want to attract and how you're
going to communicate externally to get their attention and leverage your
company as the best place for them.

Deciding where to work is an emotional decision. According to
LinkedIn (2015), the most important factors for accepting a new job are
compensation (49 percent), professional development (33 percent), and
work/life balance (29 percent). Each of these factors is emotional because
each has a massive impact outside of the office. Compensation determines
whether someone is able to send their child to college or go on vacation.
Professional development determines how successful you can be and how
far you can go in the company. Work/life balance is essential for mental
health and burnout.

When getting attention for your brand as an employer, begin with
the feelings you want your employees to have. Figure 2.1, adapted from
Robert Plutchik's Emotion Wheel (Hallett and Nguyen 2021), highlights
the most basic emotions, such as joy and anger, and then breaks them
down further into more complex emotions. Debate the pros and cons of
each one and how they fit into your business. At the end of the day, you
should agree on three to five feelings you want to create. These become
similar to values. The best companies will evaluate everything they do
internally and externally based on whether they create these feelings.
Every photo, every blog post, and every job description should help
connect with potential employees emotionally, especially when shared
through your company's social media channels. These become the "true
north" for the employer brand. If a potential employee is perusing your
company's LinkedIn page before the interview and doesn't see thoughtful
inclusion of employee culture on the feed, it may give them pause.

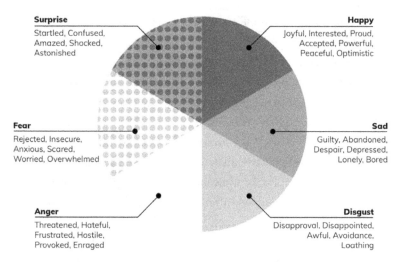

Figure 2.1 Wheel of emotions

Centers of Influence

There can be great business value in creating and executing marketing campaigns solely focused on referral sources. So how can companies attract awareness from centers of influence? The answer is top-of-mind marketing.

Think about the last time someone asked you for a referral. Perhaps they needed a new accountant or lawyer or massage therapist or landscaper. What did you do? Chances are you thought of someone with whom you had a great experience or relationship. The experience could have been recent, or if it was truly spectacular, it could have been in the distant past. Most people suggest the one, two, or three companies that they think of first. Even if they had an amazing experience at a hotel on their honeymoon 20 years ago, they are more likely to recommend a hotel they stayed at more recently even if the stay was good, not great. That is because they have confidence it is still just as good as when they visited not long ago.

There are some basic principles for top-of-mind marketing in order for it to work well:

- **Simplicity**—If you are going to depend on someone else to get attention for your brand, it must be simple for them to explain what you do. Even if Twitter is not your channel of choice to engage this audience, consider keeping your message tweet-length for the sake of brevity. Too often, companies try to communicate all of their messages, as complicated and technical as they may be. While a customer might understand the nuanced difference between an electrical and self-actuated valve, the business coach carrying the message might not. Simple language, particularly when communicated in a single sentence, is critical for someone else to get attention on your behalf. Think about explaining your message to a fifth grader. Most newspapers are written at that reading level. That is because most adults can understand it even when the issue is complex or complicated. Some marketers argue that the integrity of the message might be sacrificed if they make it too simple. They may be right. But remember that there will be opportunities to create engaged and converted attention once awareness exists.

- **Clarity**—In our example, the person asking for the referral is looking for the best options and turning to a trusted source because they believe this person would know best. Once they hear a recommendation, their next question is often about other providers. "Are they like [competitor A]?" "What makes them better than [competitor B]?" Your centers of influence need to be able to answer these questions in order to get you the attention you need. Creating an FAQ e-mail that you send to referrers every now and then can help with this, and so can conversations with your salespeople. Marketing can support sales here once again by using e-mail automation to set up regular networking calls and meetings with centers of influence. In those meetings, they provide a really clear and short document with just a few things to know to make a great referral. They can also send this document as a follow-up e-mail so it's searchable and easy to forward to someone else. Preparing social media toolkits with precomposed social posts for these advocates to share is a nice complement to the e-mail.

- **Consistency**—Communication with referrers should not be limited to times when there are gaps in the sales pipeline. There should be a plan in place to send them new and different content every few weeks. This could include intentional social media posts they can easily share, information on events or webinars, and educational videos they can use to help others. All of these things arm people responsible for "word-of-mouth" with something specific to share on your behalf.
- **Community**—The best way to get attention from someone else's network is to collaborate with them, forming a shared community. Co-writing an e-book, cohosting an event, inviting a referral partner on a podcast, or sharing a trade show space are all great ways to make it easy for others to promote you to their networks. Nothing says trust and credibility like partnering together to do something that helps you both.

In 2014, we began hosting Social Media Day in Philadelphia. It has become the largest event for digital marketing professionals in the area and has grown so much that it is now its own nonprofit organization. In the beginning, it benefited Slice Communications by helping us generate brand awareness for who we are and what we do. It also helped us get connected attention from people who signed up to learn more about it and of course, we generated quite a lot of engagement from people who attended. However, the biggest benefit we received is from our centers of influence. We have featured many of them as speakers, panelists, and moderators at the conference, which has given them reasons to promote us to their communities. Hopefully, we are also top-of-mind whenever someone asks them about a PR, social media, or e-mail marketing company. So far, the results prove that this works.

Investors and Donors

For some businesses, the most important audience is investors. These are the people who give you the capital you need in order to grow and thrive. Sometimes they are the people who buy your company. And sometimes they are the people who donate to your nonprofit. Of course, there are shareholders for publicly traded companies, but for the purposes of this book, we are going to focus on the first three mentioned since there are people much smarter about traditional investor relations.

Regular communication with your investors is essential to maintaining strong relationships. The best investors also become the biggest advocates. They benefit from you getting attention from other investors, customers, employees, and strategic partners. In all our years, we have never seen a marketer put together a plan focused just on investors. Some investors have marketers who develop plans to market companies, but not the other way around. Designing a marketing plan to reach investors can be similar to creating a plan to connect with centers of influence. However, we recommend being more direct with investors. They can only win if they help you grow. We recommend developing a weekly communication to your investors with information about how your investors can support you.

For instance, let them know about an event you are hosting and ask them to invite people they know. Tell them about an employee that you want to hire, the qualities you are looking for in that person, and where you are looking for them. Ask them to share a job listing with their social network. Let your investors know who your active centers of influence are. Chances are, you may travel in the same circles and have contacts in common. If investors know the people who have been powerful figures to grow your business, they may be able to introduce you to others like them. If there is one thing that we know about investors, it's that they are constantly surrounded by business consultants and people who provide professional services.

We once worked with a health care client who was backed by venture capital investors. These investors also invested in other health care startups. Even though our client knew the industry, players, and many of the decision-makers, they were still too hesitant to ask for the help they needed. They were too insecure to provide materials to the investors to pass along information about who they were and how they could better serve patients.

One day, they saw another company in the same investor's portfolio obtain a big media placement about a huge partnership with a hospital system. This made the client jealous, yet also pushed them to change their marketing plan to leverage the investor's clout. Things were never the same for that company. They realized that with the help and support of their biggest advocates, they could achieve their goals much more quickly and efficiently—all they had to do was ask. It also provided them—and us—with more deals and partnerships we could promote.

There comes a time in many business owners' lives when they decide that they want to sell their company. They have worked their whole life; invested blood, sweat, and tears into their business; and envisioned a future where they would be able to turn their investment in the business into cash to support their future retirement. However, selling a business is much harder than it seems. Acquisition investors who have the cash to purchase a company and take on its future, the skills and expertise to continue serving clients, and the wherewithal to face the challenges that often come with acquisitions are the hardest to find and most challenging to engage.

Marketing a company for sale used to be the exclusive job of a business broker. Today, acquirers complete due diligence on potential acquisition targets by reading the news, researching on LinkedIn, and signing up for newsletters before they even inquire about the company. Even if they're engaging a business broker, companies often check out their target's website, social media presence, marketing materials, media coverage, speaking engagements, and trade show presentations. Business brokers value companies more aggressively when those companies have a large following, an active segmented e-mail list, and a highly engaged audience of influencers, referral partners, and customers. For all of these reasons, business owners who are close to exiting need to prioritize marketing to investors at least two years in advance of their intended exit.

Nonprofit donors and supporters are a slightly different situation. First, it is important to realize that there are two kinds of donors. There are large institutional and foundational supporters and smaller, individual supporters. The large institutional sponsors are always seeking good stories to share with their audiences to show that they are supporting their local communities. They need feel-good stories. They need amazing images. They need the opportunity to showcase their corporate social responsibility plan to communities that matter to them. They also need opportunities to engage their employees and provide volunteer events.

Marketing to these large institutional sponsors means providing a regular stream of these inspiring stories, photos, and opportunities for promotion throughout the year. It also means promoting and engaging with them on social media, and using your social channels to amplify the work that they are doing in partnership with your nonprofit. These are all things that these investors care about.

Foundations are a little different and require a slightly more nuanced marketing approach. They still want great human-interest stories to showcase to their donors. In some cases, they like to share their involvement on their social channels. On the other hand, others, especially family foundations, prefer to keep a lower profile. Marketing to them effectively means more one-to-one communication, such as e-mails and phone calls. It also means giving them full reports of how their money was spent. Treat these reports as marketing materials, not just program updates. Reports are your opportunity to demonstrate how the foundation's contribution was well spent in the past, and make the case for why it's worth it to continue investing in the future. Your social channels should also reinforce this messaging, so wherever foundations encounter your business, they get a consistent message.

Keeping individual donors engaged and converted requires much more communication. First, they need to be recognized and personally thanked for their donations. You can often do that using e-mail marketing and e-mail automation techniques, but you can complement them with social media spotlight posts. This public display of appreciation on social media will encourage other followers to do the same. Individual donors also want access to special information, both to feel part of the "in crowd" and to share with others. Quite often, their motivation for donating (or renewing a donation) is to feel good about themselves. Encourage those feelings by making them feel like their voice counts. Ask them to follow you on Facebook or Instagram and leave you comments. Let them know in advance about campaigns and fundraising efforts. Offer them "sneak peek" and special event access. Send them e-mails discussing the impact of their donation, and give them an opportunity to provide suggestions and make connections for you. Doing all of this will make them feel like part of the team. More importantly, it will create an emotional connection between them and the nonprofit organization, and there is nothing like an emotional connection to keep people converted.

Partners and Suppliers

Very few businesses these days go at it alone. Many have partners, suppliers, or joint ventures with others to market and sell their products most effectively. These three groups are incredibly important to the success of organizations, particularly in a market that is challenged by external and economic factors.

Intel is a great example of a brand that has generated significant awareness over the years. Intel has one of the most famous ingredient marketing campaigns of all time. They have worked with organizations like Dell, Hewlett Packard, and other computer manufacturers who invested heavily in marketing. Intel's approach was to support those marketing efforts and be included on television and in other advertisements. Leaders at Intel knew that if they could associate themselves with these bigger consumer computer brands, they would be much more likely to create demand and awareness for their product and the value that it adds.

Today, many other companies model themselves after Intel's ingredient marketing campaign. Comarketing dollars can provide significant returns when you put them toward a strategy that aligns with an aware audience and marketers who focus on the impact they are generating. However, there has been a lot of competition for ingredient marketing because people know that it works efficiently.

So, how do you get a major brand that invests heavily in advertising to choose you for an ingredient brand for comarketing? It all begins with relationships. You must also have a thoughtful, intentional, well-financed marketing plan in order for these brands to choose you for an ingredient comarketing plan. This requires that you invest in your brand awareness so that major brands understand that you are not entirely dependent on theirs. You must be willing to push them to try new things, and you must be willing to take the risks that they are taking. Finally, you must be willing to spend at least as much time cultivating those relationships as you are on the money for the ad spend.

Advertising is not the only avenue for comarketing today. Combined PR efforts, e-mail marketing, and even social media may play a part in attracting media attention or communicating with both companies' audiences. Social media, in particular, can get complicated because of the challenge of balancing ingredient comarketing goals against priorities that may already be in place for a company's Facebook, Twitter, and Instagram pages (for example, the job descriptions we discussed in Chapter 1). Social media managers and marketers need to discuss clear expectations and strategy in order to use social media as a comarketing tool.

One of the most important lessons from COVID-19 and the economic shutdowns that occurred as a result is the importance of communication with suppliers. Many companies suffered because they were not able to obtain the supplies they needed to create their finished products. Consider Pfizer, which had the ability to create a vaccine and produce it for millions of people in late 2020. However, they were not able to scale their supply chain efficiently enough to meet the demand that existed for the vaccine. Many organizations struggle because they do not have connected and engaged attention from suppliers and potential suppliers.

As the leaders of a certified woman-owned business, we have had the opportunity to meet and speak with many people in Supplier Diversity and procurement at major companies over the years. One of their big struggles is finding enough small and small diverse businesses to supply their global operations. This is a two-way street, yet many small and small diverse businesses do not know how to market to large corporations. Cass has actually written an e-book entirely on that topic and all the digital disconnect, which is available on Slice Communications' company website. There is also a challenge for procurement professionals and supply chain professionals in terms of locating and identifying marketing to those who could supply them with the critical products and services that they need to make sure that their business continues to operate. They have had little to no marketing support. As a result, it is on their shoulders to research and find suppliers, but it does not need to be that way.

Instead, if they were to develop a marketing campaign that begins with generating attention and awareness from their potential suppliers, they would have the opportunity to build a robust database that is useful when it comes time to scale up quickly. They also need to communicate that their company prioritizes small and diverse businesses. This includes communicating this message to their primary suppliers so that those suppliers can go out and find second-level suppliers that are small and small diverse. For some companies, making the right suppliers aware of these opportunities is the single most important aspect of being able to grow.

Competitors

Can competitors be a primary targeted audience? Of course they can, particularly in industries where innovation and user acquisition are the name of the game. In the private sector, think about startups that are entering a market dominated by large, multinational companies. We worked with one such company a few years ago. They had a really innovative product to test for contamination in food products. Their intellectual property was well-protected by patents. They had investors that were dedicated to their success as well as supporting economic development and scientific communities in their area.

Consumer packaged goods companies, food manufacturers, wineries, and breweries all wanted the product because it was faster and cheaper than what the "big guys" could offer. Sure, our client wanted more customers, but sales was doing its job and the company was growing quickly. What they really needed was attention from their competitors, because they knew that the competitors would be the most likely to buy the company for a higher price than a private equity group or some other acquirer.

For that reason, they focused on delivering their corporate message about their growth, their intellectual property, and their innovative discoveries through business media and speaking opportunities. They knew their competitors would be at all the same conferences they attended, so they needed a position of prominence to show they were to be respected. Getting coverage in major media, including *The New York Times*, demonstrated to their competitors and others in the industry that they had something truly differentiated to offer and that there was significant value in it.

At the end of the day, the company did sell to a competitor for a price that satisfied the founders, investors, and employees. They became a startup and venture capital success story in their area and their industry.

They did this by prioritizing marketing communications focused on their competitors, which is not always the obvious choice.

When thinking about competitors, consider the five types:

- **Direct**—These are the companies that do basically the same thing you do for the same targeted audience. It can be very good to have direct competitors because they have proven a market and demonstrated a need for a product or service. Having a clear set of direct competitors can also make a marketing strategy easier to develop. It becomes easier to identify a customer audience when you know that those people are likely to be following or engaging with the competitor. It can be easier to develop a positioning strategy when it is clear which companies yours needs to position against. And in some cases, like the previous story indicates, it can be clear to everyone involved where there is an opportunity for acquisition. Of course, in some markets there are hundreds or even thousands of direct competitors, which can make positioning difficult. We recommend picking the three or four most prominent and focusing on them. Follow them on social media, sign up for their e-mail newsletters, put Google alerts on their company names and the names of their CEOs. Doing all this will help inform your marketing strategy and ensure that it is adjusting to changes competitors and the market are experiencing.

- **Indirect**—There are companies out there that do something slightly different than what you do and are taking a share of the market from you. Our industry is a great example of that. We provide PR, social media, and e-mail marketing services. There are a lot of companies that provide website design, digital advertising, and search engine optimization. They do not do what we do exactly, but clients may decide to invest in a new website instead of spending money on social media this year. This is incredibly typical. It also makes marketing strategy a little more difficult because it requires education about what makes your products and services better than other, different products and services. There is an educational component that must be part of the plan when most of the competitors are indirect.

- **Perceived**—This is often the most overlooked type of competitor. These are companies that do not do what you do at all BUT customers and industry don't realize that. Imagine that you are in the compliance services business. No, most people don't know what that even means, so don't overthink it. There is a perception that because compliance is a "legal thing," a law firm would be the best provider of these services. That is not the case at all. It is a different type of service that law firms don't do. In fact, they usually refer the business out to compliance service firms because they have no knowledge or capacity to handle the challenge of ensuring a financial services firm is compliant with regulations issued by the Securities and Exchange Commission. In complex and niche markets, perceived competitors are the most prominent and hardest to position against since there are extremely low levels of awareness and understanding.

- **Partner**—Partner competitors are the most common competitors for nonprofits. These are organizations that often work together to achieve a goal. Because they are achieving similar missions, there is competition for donors, both large and small. The same is true for organizations that depend on distribution partners or joint ventures. They work together sometimes, and they compete for clients, market share, and donations other times. This competitive landscape can be the toughest for a marketing strategy because it cannot put down the competitors, it cannot undercut pricing, and it cannot undermine the relationship. Instead, it must be thoughtful and supportive. Most often, we recommend a strong focus on creating engaged attention with audiences where partner competitors dominate the conversation.

- **Aspirational**—Many small and emerging companies are not even considered to be on the same level as their competitors, but they want to be. Identifying a clear set of organizations that you want to compete with can give the marketing team a very clear direction and make decisions about the marketing strategy easier. Often, the focus of this strategy is all about awareness from the aspirational competitors' audiences. The good news is that "punching above your weight" is very doable from a digital perspective where the playing field tends to be more level and a company can make steady progress running toward the end zone.

Over the years, we have worked with more than one CEO who has told us that their company is so innovative and different that they do not have competitors. They are lying to themselves and others. There is no such thing as an organization that does not have competitors. If you are having a hard time figuring out who your competitors are, ask these questions:

- Who is getting the attention I want to get?
- Who is getting the money I want to get?
- Who is getting the credibility I want to get?
- Who is getting the thought leadership recognition I want to get?
- Who is getting the speaking opportunities I want to get?
- Who is getting the referrals I want to get?

If nothing else, you have competition for attention. Once you understand this, developing a plan that gets that attention will be much easier.

CHAPTER 3

How and Where to Find People

Your business interacts with a lot of people every day. The people who are currently connected and interacting with you are the most important group that matters to the success of your business. But how many of them are engaged in your social media presence? Probably not many. This is one of the biggest mistakes organizations make. They focus on getting new followers instead of starting with those who are already part of their communities. We will discuss attracting new people in more detail later, but the best thing to do is start by paying attention to people who already have a vested interest in your business.

Your employees should be your biggest fans. If they are not, you may have bigger issues to address than how many followers you have on LinkedIn or Facebook. But that's a problem for another book. Let's assume that your employees care about your organization and want it to succeed. How many of them are part of your social media community? It may seem strange to ask your employees to follow you, but consider: There is no one better to share your news, celebrate your wins, and support your campaigns. Employees are connected with each other, your customers, your prospective employees, and many others in your industry. People in your employees' network may be the ones that bring you the next big idea or deal.

One way to find and engage employees is to begin when they are still applicants. Automated messages in response to them submitting a resume should encourage them to follow you on social media and include links to the channels. The recruiters you use—internally or externally—should ask applicants if they have reviewed and followed your company's social media presence. If applicants have not, recruiters should recommend it.

Following the channels should be part of the onboarding process for new employees, something they just do automatically on their first day.

Another strategy we have found incredibly effective is to celebrate employees on their first days, anniversaries, and when they have significant accomplishments. Adding these to your editorial calendar will increase the likelihood that employees will follow and engage with your posts. Doing this has the added benefit of signaling that you care about and celebrate the people who contribute to your business. This is always a good thing to do, even if an employee leaves weeks or months later. A steady flow of employee-focused content will significantly increase your following.

If employees in your organization do not engage with social media, it is likely that they are unsure of how to use it or afraid they will do something wrong. The best way to address this is training. There are many benefits to offering social media training sessions to your employees at all levels. Many workers stay at companies because they have professional development and growth opportunities. Teaching them about social media is an easy way to check that box. On top of that, you can get them to start following and sharing in each and every session. They have an opportunity to ask questions and make suggestions about how the company can communicate better with others like them. They may even become advocates for their colleagues to get involved in promoting the company on social media.

A quick note about training and engaging your employees in the social media effort: this always works best when there is a clearly defined social media policy in place. If you do not currently have an employee policy, there are many examples and templates available online. The most important thing is to focus on what people *can* do and not what they *cannot* do. Ensure that introducing the social media policy is part of the onboarding process, offer trainings on it regularly, and update it annually. This will indicate to your employees that social media matters and that they can be part of the company's growth in that area.

Customers are the next important group you know and need to convert to social media followers. There are a number of ways to do this. Begin with the research stage. When clients and customers research you, they often look at your website first. Make your social media channels prominent on your website, and there is no doubt more people will follow you. Of course, the benefit is that you will be more likely to stay connected and top-of-mind with them. Many prospective clients also include social media channels in their research phase, whether they are buying services or products. They want to get a better understanding of the organization beyond the website, and social media channels provide that. Whether you use an automated shopping cart abandonment e-mail or a presentation to the executive suite, your sales and marketing teams should make promoting the channels part of everything they do. That said, there needs to be something relevant, insightful, actionable, or inspiring on the channels when they visit.

If you don't have a customer list with e-mail addresses, you may want to rewind your efforts a bit and gather this data in order to lay the foundation: you need to have this essential infrastructure in place in order to make the most of your social media marketing campaigns. This database with e-mail addresses is critical for a whole series of marketing tactics, including e-mail marketing and social media. Once you have it in place, you have the ability to create custom audiences in many social media channels. On your business page, you can access advertising mod-ules that enable you to upload your list of contacts and send promoted messages to them through social media channels. This will significantly increase your effectiveness in getting your customers to become part of your online community. Your e-mails delivered to their inbox should complement the messages they see from your brand while scrolling through their feeds.

Once your customers are becoming engaged with your social media channels, do whatever you can to promote them and your relationship with them. Share their posts (as long as they are relevant to your audi-ence), celebrate their wins, promote their thought leadership, and reuse their content (with their permission). As long as you're citing your cus-tomer as the originator of the photo or video you'd like to share, requesting permission isn't legally mandatory. That said, it's an excellent opportunity to create a more personal, human connection with your audience. Thank them for their post and ask them if you could share it, while giving credit to them, of course. If they have not yet followed you for whatever reason, they will once they know that you are supporting them.

Investors and partners are the final group of people you already know that should be part of your social media community. For most companies, getting investors engaged is easy. They have a very clear incentive for helping you promote your business. In most cases, they just want to know what your plans are. On a quarterly basis, talk with them about what you are doing on social media and how they can get involved. This is particularly important if you are fundraising or looking to bring on additional investors. Many investors know others, and they tend to be connected online. Every time they share something your organization is doing—or even if they just leave a comment—your messages get to their audiences. More importantly, your association with and support from them becomes public and obvious in the moment and for the days and weeks to come. Anyone doing research into your company will likely see that support from your investors and it will benefit you.

Partners, such as suppliers and referral partners, are often the easiest to convert into online followers. They are often in the business of selling and marketing themselves, so they "get it." They want to sell to you or receive referrals in return, so they have a natural incentive to respond to you. However, businesses rarely ask these partners to follow and engage. Try this with your suppliers instead: Every time you post something about them, their products, or their services, send them a quick e-mail with a link to let them know. Ask them to share, and let them know you will return the favor. You will find that your social media following starts growing with the right people.

Another way to leverage your existing business connections for social media is to create content together. Let's imagine a law firm sends you a lot of business. You could easily host a webinar together and both promote it on social media. There is no doubt they—and some of their connections—will start following you.

For another example, let's say a logistics and transportation company helps you get your products to customers. Create a video or photo slideshow highlighting both companies working together to get the product in the hands of people who need it. Put yourself in the shoes of a baker or the locally-owned dairy company that supplies milk and butter. You can easily celebrate most suppliers on any social media channel with a simple photo and quote that promotes both their company and your own. In every one of these situations, your social media community will grow.

Once you have "found" the people you know and gotten them engaged in your organization's social media community, the next step is to turn to new people. So where do you find them? You and your team meet new people every day. Working your social media channels into everything you do will give them an opportunity to connect with you. Even if there's no business to be done now, you will benefit from staying top of mind with them. We have worked on deals for two, four, six years, all the while continuing to send social media posts and e-mails designed to ensure that when it was time for them to hire an agency, they remembered us.

Take a moment to think about where you can incorporate your social media channels into your marketing, sales, and customer service processes. Get the team together and do an audit of every touch point you have with your priority audiences. Once you have done that, find the easiest places to update and include mentions of your channels. These mentions can be graphics, images, audio, videos, or writing. You can simply list your channels, or you can express why people should follow you. You can also incentivize it, which we'll explain in more detail later in this chapter.

Here are some examples of areas where other companies have tied social media to their marketing and customer service messaging:

- Auto-replies to website messages
- Client contracts (permission to post)
- Order confirmation e-mails
- Customer service calls and online interactions
- Phone call hold messages
- Invoices
- Reports
- Purchase orders
- Customer surveys
- New applicant messages
- Waiting room displays
- Brochures and other marketing materials

- Industry/conference presentations
- Billboards
- Promotional items

The list can be extensive. Remember, every interaction is an opportunity to get and stay connected with your audiences, which then is an opportunity to start or continue a conversation.

Beyond these free, organic promotional opportunities, there are also paid and promoted opportunities to find and attract new people. Facebook, Instagram, LinkedIn, and Twitter change their paid advertising platforms constantly, so it doesn't make sense to write about the specifics of them in a book. The social media companies themselves maintain online resources with details on paid advertising plans. When it comes time to launch a social media ad campaign, refer to them.

The underlying philosophy behind developing a paid social media ad strategy should not change. It begins with using demographics and psychographics to create a detailed profile of your target audience, as we covered earlier in this book. In some cases, it can help to have a specific example of your ideal audience in mind for your ad campaign. To use an example audience that we know *very* well, let's say you're trying to target us—the authors of this book. You can target people who live in the suburbs of Philadelphia, have a son, work in marketing, and are interested in gardening (Dana). Or you can target people who went to The Catholic University of America, enjoy Cherry Coke Zero, and read *The New Yorker* (Cass). Finding the right people through social media advertising in order to get the largest community and best return on your investment requires that you really understand them and are honest with yourself about how you can make their lives better.

However, if you choose to go this route and build a paid campaign to reach new audiences, we should warn against "paying to increase followers for followers-sake." Most social media platforms will ask you to choose an objective before building out a campaign, and it may seem attractive to focus on getting new people to "like" or "follow" your company's page. Push yourself to ask why. Do you want to increase brand awareness with prospective customers? Do you want to focus on deepening engagement with your audience? Select an objective that considers the people behind the profiles and how you want to interact with them, rather than thinking of adding to the "follower count" in your monthly reports.

Too often, we work with companies who think marketing messages about their products and services will make people want to talk with them, through social media or otherwise. This is rarely true. Real-life, actual human beings want to know why your product or service matters to them. This is what will get them to join your community. Consider what you say in these ads. Are you speaking to the audience in a meaning-ful way or just screaming through a loudspeaker hoping someone hears? Do the words you use sound like the audience and communicate what it's like to do business with you? How do the images you use communicate your value or help the audience self-identify? What feeling do the ads cre-ate (e.g., excitement, calm, confidence, fear)? Once you know all of these things, you are ready to spend money on social media to find the right people who will help your business grow.

Remember when we mentioned your customer list a few pages back? That list can be used to generate a "lookalike audience," which is an ad type most social media platforms offer. You upload your list of e-mails into the system, and the channel finds people like those on your list based on behaviors, interests, and other activities on the platforms. This can be a highly targeted way to get people a lot like those you already know and who already know you.

Over the years, our company has designed many special campaigns and promotions designed to help companies find new people. Or, more accurately, to help new people find companies. We have also witnessed many that have failed in this objective. There is a basic rule that can be applied to all social media contests: The perceived value of the prize must be significantly higher than the perceived value of the action the person must take to win it. With this in mind, stop offering free iPads as prizes. Instead, think about what your audience really wants.

Years ago, we were working with a magazine that had launched a new health and fitness—focused website and social media channels. The team at the magazine thought they would get people to nominate their "health heroes" for a chance to win a basket of health products. They were wrong. Writing a nomination takes time and thought. It can be a lot of work just for a prize that was basically some free samples.

We rethought the contest quickly. Health and wellness leaders are human beings. They are doctors, nurses, athletic trainers, nutritionists, yoga instructors—you get the point. What did the magazine have that they would all really want? A full-page profile, of course! The actual cost of the prize was extremely low for the magazine, but buying a full-page ad in the magazine could cost fifteen thousand dollars. There was a perception that the value of the prize was extraordinarily high. As soon as we launched the competition, hundreds of the right people started applying and nominating others. The campaign was a massive success in helping the brand connect with new people—actual human beings who care about the same thing. If you are planning to host a competition or giveaway, first understand whether it will resonate with your current audience and people like them. If not, spend your time and money elsewhere.

You may be thinking, what about influencers? How can they help me find people? That's a big topic, and we will address it in Chapter 6: How People with Influence Can Help.

CHAPTER 4

Why Listening Matters

We're sure you have been at a party at some point where you got stuck in the corner talking to somebody, and by "talking," we mean listening while someone rattled on and on without taking a breath while you politely nodded. No matter how hard you tried to get out of the conversation, you couldn't escape. That's what most businesses are doing on their social media channels today. We're just talking and talking, and it doesn't seem to matter whether anyone listens, responds, or even cares what we have to say. Our audiences may just be politely nodding in the corner. Why does this happen? Because many businesses have not put in the effort to understand what people really want to hear. That's where listening comes in.

There are two basic types of listening: active and passive listening. Active listening is a form of listening that drives immediate, meaningful interaction. This can mean identifying opportunities for your brand to join an ongoing conversation in a meaningful way, or responding to someone who's reached out to begin a conversation with you. The other type of listening is passive listening, which is a broader approach to observing people's behavior. Companies use passive listening to determine sentiment and inform future posts, events, messaging strategies, and other forms of content and connection.

Performing both active and passive listening effectively requires a lot of work. It also requires dedicated resources, so in both cases, we recommend that people put social media listening tools in play. These are technology platforms that monitor certain handles, channels, and keywords to help you understand what people are saying about companies and brands on the Internet. Putting these tools in place and making adjustments to help them work well will make both types of listening much easier.

If you are not sure what type of social listening platform is right for you, that's understandable! There are many different options out there, and they change all the time. We recommend that companies conduct an Information Technology Request for Proposal every 12 to 18 months to ensure that they have the most up-to-date and effective social listening platforms in place. Yes, there is some expense to include this technology in your company. Usually, social listening tools operate on a subscription basis. But using these insights will greatly inform your marketing and communication strategy, not only on the social media front but across the company. It is a relatively inexpensive way to conduct market research and ensure that you're listening to conversations you need to hear from your customers, employees, and other communities that matter to you. Doing this will encourage people to keep driving and contributing to conversations about strategy and messaging across your company.

Active Listening

Active listening is how you initiate a conversation or engage in an existing one that someone from your audience initiated. Active listening should lead to immediate interaction. It can drive meaningful conversations. It can make your customers feel cared for. It can help shift the balance for people who may have become detractors to potentially be neutralized, or even become advocates. Active listening also ensures that you have access to qualitative data you can use to drive decision making.

Conversation Openers

The single most important thing that you should be doing on your social media channels right now is responding to people who are trying to have conversations with you. Of course, this includes basic, timely customer service—which most people expect from B2B brands. But the definition expands beyond just answering questions.

A while back, we started working with a food-based franchisor. When we first logged into their Twitter and Instagram accounts, we found hundreds of messages that had gone unanswered. These messages included questions about locations of stores where people wanted to go and buy things, questions about hours of operation, and complaints about stores and products. They also included messages from people sharing how much they loved the product, the stores, the company, and the brand. All of these are conversation openers. They are invitations from people to have an interaction or a back-and-forth. And each and every one of these conversation openers is an opportunity to grow and expand the brand. In some cases, they are also opportunities to protect and reinforce the brand. However, many companies don't keep an ear out for people who are trying to interact with them.

Many years ago, Cass got in a terrible car accident. At the time, she had a wonderful Ford Fiesta that she absolutely loved. She was sitting at a red light, and somebody came from behind and smashed their car into hers. Cass was actually headed to a fundraiser and her car was full of refreshments for the students working at this fundraiser. When the other car hit her, the soda and the juice exploded into the front windshield of her car from the trunk. It was an immediate moment of panic—she wasn't sure if she had lost control of her bladder or even if her eyeballs had popped out, as strange as that sounds! It turned out that the person who had hit her was on drugs and had stolen the car, and they didn't even realize she was there when they ran full speed into the back of her car. Luckily, Cass was okay.

Cass sent a message to Ford, thanking them for making such an amazing car that kept her safe in such a horrible accident. Believe it or not, she never heard back from Ford. They were actually running a type of user-promoted or influencer campaign at the time, focused on the benefits of the Fiesta. They spent a lot of money on it. And here Cass was, talking about how great the Fiesta was, with a picture of her damaged car, but with her smiling and happy. This was a lost opportunity for the company to engage with somebody who wanted to be an advocate and share a story about their car's safety.

Conversation openers must be heard. Whether they are positive, negative, or neutral, somebody is trying to talk to you through your brand presence on social media. You must be aware when this is happening, and you must have a plan to interact in ways that can benefit you.

Interceptions

A second form of listening that all companies should be doing is listening for interceptions. This type of listening requires that you set up keyword monitoring for certain words and phrases. First, you want to make sure that you are always looking for your brand names and the names of all of your products. Even if somebody doesn't tag you or comment on one of your posts, you want to be aware of any time that people are talking about you online or on social media. They might just be mentioning you without trying to open a conversation, but it doesn't mean that they are closed off if you happen to catch their post. Depending on the original mention of your brand, you may be able to reply, ask for a testimonial, or invite them to share feedback. You have an opportunity to intercept the conversation and possibly turn it to your advantage.

The second type of interception starts with tracking keywords or phrases that are related to you or what you do. For instance, if somebody on Twitter is asking for a recommendation about a great baby bottle and you happen to be in the baby bottle business, you want to know about that question. The same is true for a lot of different products and categories. We want to know if anybody is asking for a great PR firm or social media strategist for e-mail marketing. That way, we can reach out to them and say, "Hey, we might be able to help you."

The third type of interception listening is focused on what's being said about your competition. Let's say that somebody is out there complaining about your competition because they've had a bad experience or a product didn't work the way that it should have. That's an opportunity to intercept and say, "We are sorry that you had a bad experience with them, but we are happy to help you." Doing this sort of listening will put you at a competitive advantage. It's also unlikely to create problems with your competitors, because chances are, they're not doing that type of in-depth listening in the first place. In fact, very few companies are. For that reason, you have an opportunity to gain customers and market share secretly in areas where there are high levels of competition.

Interception listening can be applied in a number of different ways as well. Let's pretend you are attending, sponsoring, or speaking at a major industry conference. If people are talking about that conference in advance, you want to know so that you can reach out and offer to meet for coffee or invite them to the session where you're speaking. Interception listening also works well if you use it to follow relevant hashtags. If you're not already familiar with them, hashtags are a way to organize information about a particular subject. Monitoring hashtags that are relevant to you provides more opportunities to intercept a conversation and to steer it to the advantage of your brand or company.

Surveys

Many people rely on surveys to gather information and improve their brands and interactions. This is a great idea, but often traditional surveys are not designed for social media. There are a couple of ways to adapt this way of listening. The first is to collect e-mail addresses and then send out surveys directly to their inboxes. With this approach, social media is an avenue to deliver your message and solicit feedback from your audience more widely. The e-mail survey itself is still an opportunity to collect in-depth feedback. You can certainly share a link to an online survey, (e.g., something built through a tool like Survey Monkey) directly on your social channels, but you may find a higher response rate when collected through e-mail. One-question "quick polls" are also a great way to get information. Of course, you might not always get organic responses to these one-question surveys if you don't already have a large, active, and engaged social media community. People aren't going to answer a survey just because you put it out there. They want to know what is in it for them or why it is easy. You can also solicit feedback in other ways. For instance, you might want to do a "leave in the comments" type of approach. This is better for open-ended, qualitative survey data that you want to collect.

Finally, you can use social media to recruit for focus groups. We've actually had a lot of success with this historically. You can use your social channels to announce that you're seeking input from your community members and give details about when, what format (virtual or in-person), and what compensation you're offering. This is an opportunity to get survey questions answered in a way that is more interactive and more detailed. A focus group gives you more qualitative information than you might otherwise get from a survey.

Each of these techniques is a chance to improve your active listening to the people that are in your social media following. We recommend that social media practitioners incorporate at least one of these techniques into their social media plan throughout the course of the year to ensure not only that they are listening to the community, but also to provide some value back to other divisions in the company.

We recommend keeping open conversation between social media practitioners and other division leaders. Social media practitioners need to listen to other department or division leaders to understand what they need to do to help support the company's growth. But as social media practitioners also develop meaningful data surveys and new ways to engage based on quantitative and qualitative feedback, then the social media team is automatically providing value within the company. That will really pay off when it comes to getting conversations going within the company. It also helps people see and feel the importance and the critical functionality of social media within the business.

Passive Listening

Do you love or hate the term "people watching?" It seems like such an obvious, even mundane activity, but for some people it holds a mesmerizing appeal. The idea that we would actually sit down and just watch people interact even shows up in dating profiles as a unique, modern way to spend time. But the truth is that we have always watched other people.

When we people watch, or perform passive listening, we are looking at how people interact with us and each other, how they talk, how they reinforce their points, how they express love and affection. As humans, we always want to understand other people. By using different social media techniques and tools, we can do incredibly powerful passive listening online. If you love people watching and work in social media, you'll probably find you enjoy this task. Passive listening (or online "people watching," if you prefer) should be part of your regular social media routine because not only will it inform what you're doing as a social media practitioner, but it can and should also inform business strategy.

Data Analysis

If you've seen Netflix's 2020 documentary-drama *The Social Dilemma*, you understand how much data social media channels are collecting and tracking on each and every person who uses these platforms every second of the day. Cass and Dana were both shocked at how many people were surprised at the data that has been collected. In today's day and age, we have access to everything you might want to know about a person, from their age to their relationship status to their summer vacation spot. There's a saying that Facebook knows that people are going to get engaged before they do. That is because of artificial intelligence, machine learning, and advanced data collection.

Marketers and social media practitioners can and should use these data collection and tracking tools to their advantage. We should do this beyond just using this data to target and deliver ads. We should use it to truly understand people. What are the unanswered questions in your company that stump the leadership team time and time again? Do they really know who the customer is and what people care about? Do they really know who influences the decision making? Do they know what other brands and influencers are out there? If not, it is time to design a data study and use social media to understand these things. It is time to develop hypotheses about your audience—the actual human beings that will help your company grow. It is time to test assumptions.

There's tremendous power in doing this type of listening, but the amount of data available to us can be overwhelming. For much of this, you may need to engage a data analyst, or someone who specializes in combing through information in order to find the actionable insights. Because it's one thing to pull reports and create graphs based on your passive listening findings—it's another thing to interpret trends and identify predictive behavior based on these findings. So many people talk about how they make data-based decisions, but is the data statistically significant, or is it just enough to lead your gut instinct in a certain direction? As social media practitioners, we have access to real data that can help drive the rest of the business, as long as we have the appropriate tools and resources to translate it.

Influencer Review

"Influencers" have influence because people listen to them. Now, there's some debate at which level people are listening to them, of course. Macro influencers can have large numbers of followers but cannot be relied on to sell a couple of t-shirts. Micro influencers can have tremendous influence over where people order dinner tonight. Associations and trade groups also have a tremendous amount of influence in terms of leading conversations in their industries. And yet we as social media practitioners rarely listen to influencers in a way that informs our campaigns, messages, and strategies. This must change.

Influencers are telling us—and the people we care about—what to care about. An influencer may impact what you buy, how you think, and where you get information. The audiences and communities we're trying to reach look to influencers they trust to guide these major decisions. If we listen to influencers, we can have better, more meaningful conversations with our communities. We will know what our communities will be thinking and talking about tomorrow and the next day, because the influencers in their sphere have power over that. And if we have conversations with influencers in our spaces, we can better strategize how to be right there in the conversation as it is happening. We can add value because we are relevant in that moment.

Relevance comes from listening to people who hold influence. It comes from analyzing what they are saying, the reactions that they are getting, and the people who are interacting with them. And because this happens over social media, it is all out there, publicly available to each and every one of us. The better we know the influencers, the better we know our audience. For that reason, influencer listening and analysis belongs in a social media plan.

Competitor Review

At our company, we have a saying that "different is better than better." The most important thing we can do with our audiences is make it clear to them how we are different from competitors and other solutions available in the market. Doing this requires that we know what the competitors are saying, what other thought leaders are sharing, and what other products are available.

We cannot know we are different if we exist in a vacuum. We must open up our listening to include our competitors. Too often, companies do a competitor review and benchmark in the very beginning of an engagement or when they are developing a three-or five-year plan, but then they never go back and look at what those competitors are saying ever again. We need to stay up to date with what competitors are sharing over social, their media coverage, and new offers they're introducing. We need to understand what is resonating with their audiences if we want their audiences to be ours.

A best practice to listen for competitors is to monitor and report on them weekly. Communicating this degree of listening internally in your company will help the sales team, recruiting, product development and R&D team, and even the legal and compliance teams. It will help pretty much everybody in the organization. We've worked with many companies over many years, and very few of them actually know what is going on with their competitors. They are way too busy just focusing on what they need to achieve on a daily basis. They can be under a tremendous amount of pressure just to do that. But unfortunately, that head-down approach can sometimes lead to a head-in-the-sand approach.

When we have a head-in-the-sand approach, we often make the wrong investments in the wrong things. We do not know where the competitors are going, and we do not know where we need to go as a result. And so this passive listening, whether or not we ever interact with any of our competitors directly, will better inform our strategies in marketing and across the business.

CHAPTER 5

How to Talk With People, Not at Them

The most important thing that we do as human beings is to communicate with each other. We could argue about what defines interpersonal relationships overall, but from a business standpoint, the most important thing we do is talk with each other. In business relationships, conversations form the basis of all of the work that we do together. It's very rare that people support each other's business without some sort of conversation, whether written or verbal, over Zoom or in person. Talking with each other is how people decide to become customers, offer or accept a job, refer business, and supply each other products we need to succeed.

A few years ago, our company hosted the head of social media from Reebok at our Social Media Day Philadelphia event. He was advocating for our advice to businesses to shift from counting likes (that is, how many people "like" you) to counting engagements (that is, how many people interact with you) on Facebook. While we understand that interactions are important, they are only important insofar as they support the creation of meaningful conversation. The more conversations you have, the more business you will have.

So, what does it mean to talk with people and not at them? When you talk with people, you begin with a conversation that you both find interesting, that gives both of you a chance to exchange ideas and add feedback to another person's point of view. When you talk with people, there is a back-and-forth where you both get to respond. We believe that great social media is about talking with people.

When you talk at people, you share what's on your mind, regardless of whether it is relevant to the other party at all. You tell someone about yourself, your family, your background, your likes, and your interests. You never stop to ask them about their thoughts on the topic or their experience.

Talking with people usually means holding space for feedback, questions, and different opinions. Let's think about this. Say you're trying to have a conversation with an audience on LinkedIn. How would you go about doing that? Sure, you can be direct and open with your business goal: "Buy my product or service, please." Even politeness isn't going to help here. You could try to frame it as a question to get some kind of valuable data from your audience ("Give us your e-mail address, please"). But most people do not interact with each other that way on LinkedIn. What you need is a powerful entry point that demonstrates you've read the room and understand the space.

A powerful ask shows that you know your community. You understand what really matters to them. You have listened to them, investigated their concerns and pain points, and you see their motivations and mindsets. When you make the powerful ask, your questions are grounded in your understanding of your audience.

As an example, let's explore two different options. In the first option, a company asks, "Do you like our car product (A) or product (B) better?" Know who's going to answer that question. More than likely, some of your employees are following you on LinkedIn and will see this post. Maybe some of your vendors are keeping tabs on your LinkedIn profile. Both of these groups have an interest in responding to that question, because they want to get something in return (e.g., positive attention from a supervisor, or a foot in the door for a deal). Chances are, they don't really care that much about product A or product B. Their motivations revolve around connecting with the company and getting some positive attention, and they think the best way to do that is to respond to the question on LinkedIn.

Let's try and ask a different question, one that's more focused on the audience. That question might go something along the lines of, "We've heard from many of you that you're worried about issue A. We want to know what our community thinks about that." You might continue by mentioning a prominent voice in that space and say, "She believes that the most important aspect of issue A is number three. Do you agree with her?" and include a few options based on what you've seen come up in other conversations about the issue at hand.

Think about what that powerful ask accomplishes. It communicates that the company belongs to a community on LinkedIn. It communicates that the company has listened to important issues. It communicates that they have listened to an influential member of that community, and finally it asks a question that invites a reaction to someone else's opinion. A powerful ask implies thoughtful consideration and actually encourages meaningful response.

It may seem subtle at first, but these two examples could not be more different. The second example is much more intentional, better targeted at the audience, and more considerate of their time and feedback. It demonstrates a level of self-awareness by taking people outside of the company into account. The company's focus goes beyond their products. They're showing interest in what people are experiencing, what they are feeling, and what they are worried about. The most powerful way to talk with someone is to answer their question, to respond to something they communicate, or to share an insight or perspective with them. It means moving deeper than a conversation someone's started online just for fun. In order to achieve this, social media professionals need to take a much harder look at what others are saying than what we want to say.

We first started talking about social media when it was a new business communications platform. The earliest pieces of advice we gave to our audience still rings true. You need to give before you get. Imagine showing up at a party and going around asking people for things. Who would do that? You'd be the most unpopular person at the party. However, if you showed up and started to show interest in what other people are talking about and meeting them where they are, you are much more likely to create a memorable interaction in a relationship. Social media is still all about people, which means it's all about relationships.

A few years ago, our company was managing social media for the Philadelphia Flower Show, one of the largest and most acclaimed events of its type in the world, having drawn millions of guests since its founding in 1829. Each year, there was an exclusive preview party for sponsors, special guests, and big donors. This is the first peek at the event, and it was an exciting moment for huge fans of the Flower Show to get a glimpse on social media before actually attending the show in person.

As the person responsible for social media that night, Cass got to attend and choose a couple of things to share with the audience on Facebook and Instagram. The theme was the 1960s. There were beautiful, jaw-dropping displays and exhibits. One of the things that she thought was most relatable was a yellow submarine made out of flowers. It was beautiful, but it was also fun. It was the kind of exhibit that was instantly memorable, and it was almost impossible to look at it and not smile as it emanated that elusive "warm and fuzzy" feeling. If Cass were talking *at* people, the social media caption that accompanied this photo would have said, "We love this beautiful yellow submarine created by so-and-so." But when physically listening to the crowd around her, Cass heard a couple of onlookers humming a familiar tune—something that really resonated with the guests at this sneak preview. So, in an attempt to talk *with* the people, the caption read, "We all live in a…."

The engagement on that post was amazing. It might have been the most engaging post of the entire Philadelphia Flower Show. Why? Because people wanted to respond. They wanted to finish the line. They wanted to share a memory and share in the joy of singing that song. Hundreds of people responded to the post. They finished the lyrics, but they also talked about how much they were looking forward to seeing the rest of the show in person. They asked how to buy tickets. They asked questions about when they could arrive, where they could park, what other exhibits used these specific flowers, and all sorts of other things just on that one, very simple post. And almost none of those things would have happened if Cass had just posted "We love this yellow submarine by so-and-so." The photo was the same, but the copy left space for people to get involved. It tied back to something that they cared about and wanted to be part of. As you think about each post that you put out, remember where it fits in the existing community conversation.

So how do you move your social media team from talking at people to starting to talk with people? The first thing is that you need to create a culture of talking with people within the company. That means ensuring that the social media team is not siloed apart from anybody else in the company. We think about social media as a coordinating media. Its job is to support the rest of the business. And we know how to do that, because at this point, we've written job descriptions for each of our social channels. So have your social media team set up meetings with all of the other critical people. Share the job descriptions for the different social media channels that you are using. Make sure that other people within the company understand that social media is a critical part of supporting business growth, not just something that you do for fun or because other people told you that you should. It is a core part of the business' success.

Communicating the importance of social media to the internal stakeholders and audiences within the company should open the lines of conversation between those people and the social media marketing team. The social media marketing team should be meeting with the departments or leaders that they support. For instance, if the primary goal of social is customer service, then the social team should be talking to customer service. The primary goal is to support brand awareness and move more people into the sales funnel. If the goal is recruiting, then they should meet regularly with the recruiting team, HR team, or any external recruiters working with the company. If the goal is to generate more investors or more donors, then obviously the social media team should be talking to the investor relations team or the head of development.

These conversations should be highly structured, and the social media team should spend 90 percent of those conversations listening. Making time for these conversations regularly will help the social media team better understand the targeted audiences. And that will mean that they are better suited to talk with them and not at them.

To make the best use of these conversations, here's what social media practitioners should ask, whether they meet with other key departments weekly, monthly, or every quarter:

- What does the audience care about right now?
- What are they interested in?
- What conversations are happening with that audience right now?
- Where are there opportunities to interact in person with these audiences?
- Who's influencing decision making with those audiences?
- Where are our competitors making progress with those audiences?

Social media managers should also learn about the most frequent conversations that each division lead is having with their target audience. Recurring questions or feedback, or a sense of what the audience is worried about, can inform and dramatically change everything that you put out on social media. You want to move beyond talking at people based on what the marketing team wants you to talk about in your posts. Talking with your audience based on insights you gain from department leads across the company will help make sure that your social media campaigns and messages are truly focused on reaching human beings.

When you're having these conversations regularly, with the support of senior leadership, the effect is transformative. You'll see a difference in how the company is speaking and presenting and sharing information externally. These conversations tend to dramatically change the types of content that the company puts out. They dramatically change the marketing department's social advertising. The shift in content and strategy is exactly where we start to see a more human-centered social media effort.

Voice and Tone

Whether people think you are talking at them or with them has a lot to do with the tone that you use in your communication. Tone applies not only to your social, but also the content you promote. If people are going to want to talk with you, your tone needs to be consistent. It's hard to talk with somebody when their tone is all over the place; cheerful and entertaining one day and somber and formal the next. It's critical to set clear guidelines in place around voice and tone for your company, and establishing tone should be one of the core responsibilities for whoever is running social media and content. If you haven't had conversations about voice or tone, stop right now, put this book down, and start to have them. Make sure that how your company is communicating, not just what it's communicating, makes sense for who you are as a brand.

Later in the chapter, we'll share one of the exercises we used to develop voice and tone at Slice for all of our clients. We hope you'll find the exercise helpful, too, but keep in mind that tone is not something that you set once and never revisit. Your team should be meeting quarterly to look at the tone that you are using. Review the posts that are getting the most interaction, conversation, and feedback. It's also important to look at the tone in the rest of your marketing and take a holistic view of how the sales team is communicating. That includes materials in sales presentations and proposals. Whether your tone is elaborate or straightforward, inspiring or matter-of-fact, ultimately, you need to create consistency from the first interaction on social media all the way through closing the deal or signing the contract.

The social media team needs to be in especially close communication with the person managing the website regarding tone. If somebody sees your post on LinkedIn and clicks through to the website only to find a landing page that sounds like it was written by a completely different company, there's going to be a disconnect. That disconnect means the loss of trust. That loss of trust will counteract any time, money, or other investment in your social media efforts so far. We've seen it happen when some companies put out social posts that are very different from what's on their website. And what that means is that they are confusing people.

Similarly, if one of the primary goals of social media is to help the recruiting team and the HR team, talk with these teams about the tone in the job descriptions. Quite often for potential employees, the job description is their first interaction with the company. If the job description communicates that the company is friendly or flexible, that there's potential for growth, that the benefits include office ping pong (!), but their LinkedIn feed is solely focused on selling products and services, there is a disconnect. Discrepancies like that can put potential employees off.

We know that people tend to do 12 steps of online research before they ever engage in a B2B sales conversation. They do even more research when they are considering a job opportunity. We know that your job is one of the most emotional decisions that you will make in your life, following who you marry and where you live. That emotionality is a critical decision factor, and if the emotion that a potential employee gets is uncertainty because what they read in the job description sounds so different from what they see on the social sites, then you are not going to make them want to work with you because you have already broken their trust.

Consistent tone is one of the strongest ways you establish trust, so it matters for everything you put out there. Public relations releases, social, website copy, job descriptions, sales presentations, and proposals should all be part of a unified voice that represents your company.

The next thing to think about in terms of tone is that it should be clear. Clarity of tone can go a very long way in terms of creating trust. As you're thinking about the words and images that you are using to communicate, it's important that people know exactly what the company is and what the brand stands for. There's no better way to do that than through clear tone (see Exercise 5.1). Companies that have a clear tone use simple language. They are straightforward. They are intentional. They know as much about what they would not say as what they would say. By creating

Your Voice and Tone

To identify your organization's voice and tone, start by selecting where your think your tone should be, in reference to the two terms on each side. From there, use the below questions to create concrete examples of your voice and tone.

Simple	2	3	Complex
Serious	2	3	Whimsical
Straightforward	2	3	Jargon-Filled
Warm	2	3	Authoritative
Educational	2	3	Entertaining
Specialized	2	3	Commonplace
Informative	2	3	Salesy
Inspiring	2	3	Matter-of-Fact
Tongue-in-Cheek	2	3	Reverent
Funny	2	3	Logical

This actor or actress would play my brand in a movie:

My brand's voice is very similar to this company's:

My brand would never use these words or phrases:

Exercise 5.1 Voice and tone exercise

guardrails in your social posts, content, website, and other materials, you ensure that clarity becomes the priority. Clarity is also about everybody getting on the same page in terms of what the brand stands for and the experience that you want to create.

The last critical piece of determining your voice and tone is basing it in your community. Use the words, expressions, images, and acronyms that the community uses. Create a connection through your language and lexicon. The use of lexicon is critically important in determining and staying true to your voice. Lexicon is specific to your field and persona. Most companies don't sit down and define the vocabulary, context, and connotations for the language they use. If you do pay attention to building a shared lexicon, it's going to be easy for your community to understand you, because people recognize terms and know you're talking to them. Strategic use of field-specific lexicon helps create brand familiarity, because people in your target audience will self-select when they identify the same words they use. Conversely, establish a list of words and phrases that your community would *never* use, and keep this blacklist handy when drafting posts.

The best way to start to identify your lexicon is to look at your industry trades and associations, if this is applicable. Or if you're on the B2C side, you can look at some of the biggest influencers in the space, whether they're companies or individuals. You can often take a number of posts from those communities, associations, and influencers. From there, use that material to make a word cloud. Take a little time to define the words that appear prominently in the word cloud, so that everybody on your team understands their meaning and how to use them in posts and conversations online.

CHAPTER 6

How People With Influence Can Help

If the term "influencer" elicits an eye roll, think again. There is definitely a perception of a certain type of social media celebrity whom companies pay to travel the world in bohemian fashions, or send boxes upon boxes of free products, just for the chance to be featured in a sponsored photo. In actuality, the word "influencer" has been around since 1662 (Cahn 2020). Long before anyone could have even conceived of the Internet, people looked to opinion leaders for recommendations. There has always been an appetite for this tastemaker role because it's natural to look to others for inspiration and guidance. Today's Instagrammers, YouTube vloggers, and TikTok stars are the most recent version of this role, and it's in every marketer's best interest to understand and leverage the power that they wield on their platforms.

Identifying meaningful partnerships with influencers once again comes down to understanding your audience and your overall goals. Who are you trying to reach and where do they spend their time? Who does your audience trust? And what is the call to action that you want to amplify?

Benefits of Influencer Marketing

A 2019 survey by The Influencer Marketing Hub reported that businesses made $5.20 for every one dollar spent on influencer marketing (Geyser 2021). Partnering with the right individuals can move the needle for your business, so don't doubt the legitimacy. From a B2C perspective, this could mean your chosen influencer is acting as a brand ambassador and sharing an authentic testimonial about your product or service with a call to action to "try for yourself." Often, these types of posts are accompanied by a customized promo code to encourage followers to buy in the moment.

But some of the most impactful work being done in the influencer space isn't necessarily through hard sales. Something as simple as strategic product placement can start to increase awareness for your brand. A funny stunt that breaks into the news feed but doesn't necessarily have a "buy now" call to action can arguably be effective at starting the kinds of conversations you want to have with your audience.

For instance, Anti Monkey Butt, an anti-chafing powder, wanted to expand its reach within its target market of long-haul truck drivers and farmers—generally, people whose professions induce uncomfortable sweating from long days of sitting in cabs and on tractors. After studying their audience behavior, we identified a comedian who resonated with this group and had a large following on Twitter. Dana messaged the influencer and asked if he'd be interested in trying out Anti Monkey Butt for free. We sent him a package of the powder, and he created a full video sketch joking about the seriousness of sweat in your seat. He prominently featured the product in his video and made a memorable, awareness-building piece of content that generated over a million impressions and tens of thousands of comments, reactions, and inquisitive clicks back to the site, effectively introducing the brand to more people who could benefit from the product.

Once the influencer shared his original video content, Dana thanked him profusely for his creative coverage of the product. She also asked if we could repurpose this content for our own channels. Dana was able to take a single video on Twitter and cut it for multiple channels to post organically, including running it in a targeted ad campaign. Rather than just posting links back to the product page, she was able to share truly engaging content that inspired genuine conversation in the comments.

Types of Influencers

Influencer marketing can increase sales, build awareness, and be a source of creative content—but the best campaigns start with the right personality.

It's a common misconception that influencers with a larger following will produce a higher return on investment (ROI). In reality, that's almost never the case. Although there's no universal guide to influencer level by follower count, the macro-influencer level tends to include anyone with over 250,000 followers on a single channel. These individuals are often considered celebrities on some level and can include ex-reality television stars or professional athletes. Partnering with macro-influencers is costly; in 2019, Business Insider (Taylor 2019) reported that Kim Kardashian charges half a million dollars per sponsored Instagram post—although some would consider the Kardashians a tier above as "mega-influencers." Macro- (and mega-) influencers almost always have a representative who approves partnerships and manages contracts. Statistically, their engagement rates tend to be lower—sometimes down to one-third of "smaller scale" influencers. With hundreds of thousands to millions of fans scrolling past their content, Influencer Marketing Hub reports that on average, only 1.21 percent of impressions of macro-influencer content result in some form of audience engagement (Geyser 2021). The average for micro-influencers is 3.86 percent (Geyser 2021). In short, asking a macro-influencer to post about your brand is like casting a very wide, expensive net that puts your boat on fishes' radar but may not actually reel any in.

Micro-influencers, on the other hand, are more accessible to both brands and their audiences. The unofficial range of followers is quite wide—potentially from 10,000 followers up to 250,000. Many are focused on a niche interest or industry and become experts in their space, from travel to finance to health and wellness. Because of their focus on a particular topic, they've developed meaningful relationships with their followers and established trust. You will often hear the word "authentic" used as it relates to working with micro-influencers, and this trust factor is a huge part of that authenticity. Micro-influencers understand that social media is about people. It's fundamental to success at this level. They answer questions on their posts in a timely manner. They enthusiastically respond to positive comments. There is a real investment in the community they've built. If you're not seeing this kind of engagement, as a marketer considering partnering with an influencer, proceed with caution.

Take note of the nano-influencers in your industry as well. This group of social media content creators could have only a few hundred to a few thousand followers, but they're active and trusted in their space. Think of the Facebook Group administrator who manages the conversations around niche interests, or the heavy Pinterest user who dedicated dozens of boards to an obscure topic. While it may not necessarily be costly to work with this group, marketers may need to spend more time educating potential partners on their brand as well as the expectations of the relationship. Again, there is often a sincere level of authenticity established with the community these individuals have built on their platform of choice.

It's important to consider your own colleagues and their networks as potential nano-influencers. If your goal is to recruit new talent to your organization, for instance, take a look at your existing team members and deputize the most social media savvy as company influencers. Provide them with content to share on their channel of choice, or give them a chance to shine on your company's social media channels. You could prepare a spotlight that provides some insight into their life or, better yet, give them the reins for a full takeover for a day to show "a day in the life" at your company. Then of course, ask that your in-house nano-influencer share the content on their own social channels so you're reaching their engaged network.

Even something as simple as requesting to share user-generated content on your brand's channel is an opportunity to work with a nano-influencer. Often, when a company shares a photo posted by a customer or client, that individual shares the repost in their feed. With macro-influencers (and even micro-influencers to a lesser extent) you run the risk of earning "empty" impressions from an unengaged audience. But the family, friends, and professional network following your clients and colleagues are all there because of a personal connection and therefore much more likely to pay attention to your brand in their posts.

Developing an Influencer Program: Vetting, Engaging, Setting Expectations

One of the most important questions to ask yourself when considering influencers is, "Who is already speaking to my audience?" The key is finding the conversations that are already happening in your space, rather than trying to start a new one. Instagram tends to be a popular platform for influencers, but if your audience isn't active there, search elsewhere. Look through the publications your audience reads and find the thought leaders and spokespeople in popular articles. See where they have the most robust conversations online. If your search leads you to LinkedIn, then that's where you should plan to promote your influencer partnership. The last thing you want is to invest time and money into a collaboration that feels forced just because you got approval to reach out to a TikTok influencer.

Once you've identified the platform and type of influencer you'd like to work with, research trending hashtags that are related to your brand. Of course, if you're lucky enough to have an influencer proactively engage with your brand, you can skip ahead to the vetting process. But for most organizations, this research phase is time consuming, yet critical.

Next, review your shortlist of potential influencer partners and evaluate their activity:

- **How often are they posting? What other channels do they use?** Ideally, you'll find a consistent schedule and one to two platforms that are really strong with high community engagement.
- **Are they consistently engaging with followers in the comments or sharing follower content?** If there are tons of unanswered questions or neglected comments, look elsewhere.
- **What kind of engagement are they earning?** If they have an exorbitant amount of likes with few comments, it could be a sign of fake followers or bots. Similarly, if the only comments on the posts look spammy or robotic, there's a good chance the "followers" you're seeing were purchased and therefore not the authentic community you're looking to interact with.
- **What other brands have they worked with recently?** Do these brands align with your values?
- **How often are they posting sponsored content?** If they're working with too many sponsors, it can overwhelm their audience and ultimately lower their engagement rate.

After you've vetted your candidates, reach out with your ask. It's often best to start the conversation directly through the channel via direct message. Macro-influencers are more likely to have a link for collaboration requests in their bio, so you can follow up the in-channel message with an e-mail. Much like pitching a journalist, it's customary to cite a recent piece of content that caught your eye. Demonstrate that you're familiar with their work and explain how your product or service aligns with their brand. Include your professional e-mail address and encourage to moving the conversation to that setting for additional details.

When planning your influencer collaboration, leave room for creative freedom. As content creators and experts in their space, influencers will often come to the table with their own ideas on how to create a mutually beneficial partnership. If they're open to it, set up a call to talk through their ideas and to learn what's really resonated with their community in the past.

A starting point could be proposing a co-promoted giveaway, where you provide the influencer with free products to be given away to their community through a series of posts. For instance, if your product is a health supplement, and you've partnered with a fitness influencer on YouTube, you can offer a dozen free samples to be raffled off in a contest that the fitness pro hosts from their channel. You're providing something of value directly to their community, which benefits the influencer just as much as you enjoy the exposure. Terms of the contest could involve following both your company's social channel and the influencer's channel, so you would see an increase in connections from your target audience in addition to the increase in awareness.

Much of this chapter is focused on a campaign in which an influencer posts about your brand on their owned channels. But the reverse scenario could work for certain brands, as well. Let's say you have a large community already established on Instagram, but you're trying to expand into a new niche market. If you identify a micro-influencer with a strong presence in your new target audience, you can invite this individual to take over your own channels. In doing so, the influencer would announce to their followers that they should check out your account for the duration of the takeover, which ultimately leads to new connections.

At some point in the conversation, the question of payment will arise. For certain influencers, content creation and the sponsorships associated with it are their livelihood. Many have media kits with formalized fees for different campaigns and quantity or format of posts. If you're not provided with any kind of quote, it's still not safe to assume the partnership is free.

Offering complementary products or services in exchange for coverage on their platform may be sufficient. Whatever payment is determined, it should be confirmed in writing before the campaign begins. Expectations should be clear on both ends—the type and tone of content your company anticipates, and the compensation an influencer receives for creating said content.

If money is being exchanged, we highly recommend using a contract to outline these expectations. From a federal regulation standpoint, it's also important that the influencer agrees to use appropriate language that clearly identifies the paid partnership. While these rules change from time to time, you can check the Federal Trade Commission's (FTC) most recent guidelines on disclosing relationships with brands. In most cases, using terms like "advertisement," "ad," and "sponsored" are sufficient.

In addition to compensation, discuss these expectations up front to make sure you and the influencer work together effectively:

- **Content rights**—Will you be able to use any photos or video created during the partnership in a social media ad campaign at a later date? Could you use the content on billboards? If so, how should credit be attributed?
- **Voice and tone**—Does the influencer have a solid understanding of your brand's style? What words or phrases absolutely should not be used in conjunction with your brand?
- **Workflow**—Are you comfortable with the influencer publishing content without your approval first? Who is the point of contact who will handle approvals and questions?
- **Reporting**—What kind of analytics would you like to see at the completion of the arrangement? Are you providing the influencer with a hashtag, "UTM code" for campaign reporting, or unique promo code so that you can track success on your end?

Once you have agreed on expectations for your partnership and the campaign is in motion, monitoring activity is absolutely key. If the influencer has agreed to post to their own channels directly, closely follow their content. As their audience reacts to the photos and videos being shared, find meaningful ways to engage by liking comments and inserting your brand into the conversation when appropriate. It's a delicate balance, because you still want to leave space for the influencer to engage with their own community. When in doubt, include this in the "expectations" conversation at the beginning of the partnership.

In addition to engaging on the influencer's posts, amplify all of this content on your own channels. Repost—giving credit of course—whenever and wherever it makes sense for your audience. Sharing this content with your followers adds authenticity and validity to your organization as well. Make sure you archive all content created during the collaboration. If given permission, you can repurpose this photo and video in other campaigns in the future.

Measuring Impact

When all is said and done, how will you know if your influencer campaign is a success? Revisit the goal you set for yourself at the beginning of the campaign and compare against benchmarks. If the purpose was to build awareness, how many unique people were you able to reach with the content created? If an influencer is posting on their own channels, they will need to provide this information for you. It's customary to ask for screenshots of backend analytics, especially if working in Instagram. You can ask the influencer for their own analysis: How did this content compare to other recent sponsored posts? Make sure you've kept a record of your follower count before the engagement started. Did you see a spike in followers during the campaign, meaning more of your target audience voluntarily decided to follow your account because they're interested in what you have to say? The influencer will have to share the raw data with you, which they can often do by sharing screenshots. Keep an eye on your webpage traffic during the partnership. See if there are any correlations between days and times of posts and increases in people visiting your website because they're curious about what it is you do. Ask the influencer if they also experienced a notable increase in followers. If you've been following best practices and closely monitoring the posts, you should have a good idea of the kind of engagement generated from the campaign.

Proving ROI on social media is difficult to begin with, but working with influencers introduces new challenges to this task. In addition to tracking the metrics we've just discussed, you can ask your partner to use a custom hashtag in their post and count the number of uses. If you're focused on conversion, we highly recommend providing a URL with a UTM code that's unique to your influencer so you can monitor visits back to your website directly from the campaign posts and see if anyone takes action. Retail brands are known for giving influencers custom promo codes for the same reason, so they can track usage and report on success tied to these efforts.

But the numbers only tell a small piece of the story. Beyond the quantitative report, do your own qualitative analysis by gauging the sentiment of the comments on the posts that feature your product or service. What's the conversation about? Are you seeing followers tag their friends and indicate a willingness to learn more about your company? Capturing that kind of proof that the influencer campaign is inspiring action is arguably the most valuable.

Take the Influencer Exchange Program, for instance. In 2017, Visit Philly, the Philadelphia region's official tourism marketing agency, noticed that New York City, Philadelphia, and Washington, DC were all vying for the same leisure travelers. But while they competed for the same audience, they were also prime feeder markets for one another. The Philadelphia office spearheaded a program to address this relationship: the Influencer Exchange Program, where each major metropolitan destination selected a major Instagrammer from their community to sponsor on a Northeast Corridor journey. They wanted to reach potential visitors in target markets, of course, but they were also interested in building a model that could be replicated with other destinations (and brands, for that matter).

The destination marketing organizations (DMOs) for the three cities each identified a micro-influencer on Instagram in their community with a strong local following. They developed and agreed on one joint contract that held each photographer responsible for posting at least 3 grid photos a day and 10 Instagram Story posts a day. Through connections in the hospitality industry, the DMOs secured transportation and lodging partners, which were also guaranteed (via contract) at least one post for each partner.

Beginning in September and ending in December 2017, the influencers, each with one guest, traveled to each of their nonhometown cities, spending at least two days on each trip. There were very few other guidelines given to the photographers in order to keep the content as natural and authentic as possible. And while they posted to their individual Instagram accounts, the DMOs and partners were able to repost content on their own Instagram channels as they deemed appropriate.

Without any paid boosting, the campaign earned nearly 70,000 comments and reactions. What was even more impressive, however, was the overall sentiment in the hundreds of discussions that began in the comment threads. It was gratifying to see people tagging their friends with statements like, "The trees look magical!! I need to spend more time in Philly" and "This is so beautiful! Need to book my trip to Philly and find this place."

There's no one single correct way to go about influencer marketing, which is part of the reason it's so successful. There's room for creativity, and it really leverages the fact that people just want to connect to other people at the end of the day.

CHAPTER 7

Handling Unhappy People

If this chapter seems familiar to you, it is because you may have already read a variation of it in Chapter 11 of "Pay Attention!," also written by us. This is not déjà vu! We know that this information is so central to communications we could not have you miss it, which is why we are including it in this book.

There are times in your business when you won't want attention. This is usually because some sort of crisis has occurred. Keep in mind that if you have been cultivating your social media outreach to connect with people, responding to people in difficult times is another important aspect of your social media presence. Your social media team needs a plan for how and when to use social media to speak to unhappy or angry people, whether they are dissatisfied with you specifically or expect your company to speak out on a broader crisis.

Crises fall into a number of different categories. The first are internal crises, which are things that you can potentially foresee and that you can have more control over. You often have the upper hand in dealing with these crises because you know about them first and have the most information about what happened. Examples could include a product recall, an error or problem with one of your services, a mistake with a client or a customer, financial troubles or a potential bankruptcy, or a company statement or policy that someone has flagged as discriminatory. All of these are crisis scenarios that you have the ability to fix internally.

You could call the second type of crisis an affiliate crisis. This type of crisis has a discernible connection or association with your business, but it is outside of your direct control. Consider a guest speaker you are hosting at an event who makes an inappropriate comment during their presentation. A less egregious, but still challenging crisis, could be a vendor you relied on failing to deliver in time, or providing goods or services that fall short of your company's standards and customer expectations. This level of crisis could even be a publicly known connection with an investor group, donor group, or foundation that has gotten into some trouble. These are situations where you have limited control, especially over the messaging. You don't have the same level of autonomy to steer the outcome as with an internal crisis.

The third crisis category is external crises. An example might be a *force majeure* event that interrupts your business or customers. These types of events halt the news cycle and disrupt our daily lives—like natural disasters, acts of terrorism, major financial crises, or global pandemics. You will need to react to these events in some way, but you do not have any control over them.

When you are preparing possible responses to a crisis, the most important thing to consider (in addition to the actual composition of your response) is who makes up the audience you're responding to. There are three different audiences to whom you must respond in a crisis. The first audience, and the one that is the most important, is your internal audience—your employees. In each and every one of these situations, you have to communicate with them and do it well. Unfortunately, people often overlook this because they do not think about their employees as an audience. This is a major mistake. Companies that miss this opportunity are damaging the trust that's been established between them and their employees, so be sure to prioritize internal communication first!

Crisis Communication With Employees

Your employees rely on you, just as you rely on them, to keep your business operating through the crisis. If they are uncertain what to do or fearful of what's going to happen next, it's almost impossible for them to complete their work successfully or be productive. If your company's leadership isn't providing clarity about what's going on or reassurances that you are doing everything that you can to handle the crisis, employees will begin to doubt your leadership and effectiveness. Even if leaders are communicating well with employees, you are still going to lose some productivity until the crisis resolves.

When you are not communicating with your employees through a crisis, then you actually create a communication gap, and your employees begin to look to each other for solutions or information. They may even look outside of your company. At this point, you've given up even more control in a crisis situation, and that can be detrimental because the last thing you want to do is lose what little degree of control you have in these challenging times.

It is important to make sure that you reinforce your values during a crisis, that you give your employees updates and a chance to ask questions, and that you give your management and leadership teams information to communicate with their direct reports on a more regular basis. A lot of times, people will trust information they receive from their direct supervisor or boss more than what they hear from the CEO. They have a personal relationship with the direct manager, and they know them way better than they know the CEO. So, when we think about employee communication, it really should be on a parallel path. One part is regular communication with all of the employees, and the parallel part is communication with supervisors and managers who can then share that information out to their teams. While much of this can be done through internal e-mail, consider any employee communities on social media, like Facebook groups and LinkedIn groups.

Crisis Communication With Partners

The second audience to consider when you are building your crisis communication plan is your partners. These are people who are invested in the future success of your business: your suppliers, bank or financial accounts manager, lawyer, accountant, and others that you need to continue to believe in you. They are looking to you for information and answers. They want to know what is going on because you need to work hand in hand with them to continue to deliver.

Oftentimes, we see that companies don't have a list of those contacts, let alone know which social media channels they are following the company on. When it comes time for swift, organized communication, it's often too late to begin to hunt this information down. As a result, those partners are often left in the lurch, unsure about what is happening. And that hurts trust. It also, once again, creates a communication gap, and partners will need to turn to your employees or outside sources to figure out what is going on. Your employees are not always equipped to be able to give partners the answers they need. If partners look at your external communications, the news, or other parties' messaging, this can lead to misunderstandings or even spread misinformation. Imagine your trusted vendors refreshing LinkedIn, for instance, and seeing previously scheduled posts that are now sounding quite tone deaf given the crisis.

Crisis Communication With the Public

The third audience that you definitely need to consider is your external audience. That is, everybody outside of the company, including the general public. It's not always necessary to communicate with those people during a crisis. There are times when it is better to be silent. There are times when it is better to communicate. And there are times when you can attempt to communicate indirectly.

We get asked a lot about how companies should respond when there's civil unrest, such as riots or protests. We also get asked quite a bit about how to respond to major social issues and social movements happening outside the company. It's not always important for your company to say something. Consider whether your company's voice is additive, whether it's supportive, whether it makes a difference or helps contribute to a meaningful change. If not, you may want to be quiet and save space in social media feeds for the voices that should be amplified during these times. Quiet means not only refraining from speaking about the issue at hand, but also that you should pause or take down any prescheduled posts or typical campaigns as well. What you want to avoid is appearing insensitive by going about your daily lives without recognizing that there's a major issue happening in your community or in the world.

There are other times, though, where companies do need to communicate externally. This communication cannot just happen once. You can't address a major situation with a single statement and then resume your regularly scheduled posts. If you're really going to stand up and support something, you need to prepare regular, ongoing communication, messaging, and possible initiatives. If your company cares about issues related to Black Lives Matter, or climate change, or gun control, and those issues are a critical part of your business values, then you should address them directly and communicate about them openly on your social channels.

But if your company doesn't have a dedicated and focused effort to solve those issues, and your plan is to put out a simple "thoughts and prayers" type of statement without any follow-up initiative or donation, then you are going to have a real issue. Social media can be incredibly powerful in these moments, as long as you're not being exploitative.

If your statement on a significant external issue comes without any follow-up action, people see that those words are valueless, without any real money, effort, or resources behind them. A boilerplate "We stand with…" statement also isn't necessarily connected to a company's values. It's just something that companies feel obligated to say, because they feel this external pressure that actually doesn't exist, especially on small and medium-sized businesses. So think hard as you consider what to do and what to say. Sometimes it is better to say nothing.

Instead, other options may be to communicate indirectly, and make space for the voices that do need to be heard. If some sort of external crisis is going on, and you decide that you want to make a comment on it without saying "We stand with…," or "Our thoughts and prayers are with…," there are a couple different options. For instance, if you want to make an indirect statement about Lesbian, Gay, Bisexual, Transgender and Queer+ (LGBTQ+) rights, you may have some content that you developed previously—perhaps LGBTQ+ employee spotlights or community service campaigns during Pride month. Look for past messaging that is pro-diversity and inclusion for the affected communities. Don't post on the same day or in the immediate aftermath of an external crisis, but sometime in the weeks following a significant event, you may want to republish that older content to reinforce your values. This can help people understand who you are and what you stand for in a positive way.

As you are planning your crisis communication in advance, you might want to have a meeting with your leadership team. Write out a list of potential crises (you can't anticipate everything, of course, but you can plan for some hypothetical scenarios), and then determine actions you'd take in those potential situations if they happen. How will you communicate internally? How will you communicate to your partners? In which example scenarios would you communicate externally, and would a direct or indirect statement be the best approach? Doing some of that planning will put you in a position where, when a crisis arrives, you are not at a complete loss.

Now, let's talk a little bit about crises that are of your own creation. Whether you intentionally took a risk that didn't work out, or you've encountered an unintentional error, these crises are still your problem to solve. When those come about, there are two primary golden rules of crisis response. The first is to manage your part of the crisis openly, through words and action. The second is to know the situations in which it's truly best to avoid responding.

Managing Your Part in a Crisis

The first step in managing a crisis that is of your own making is to validate concerns. If something has gone terribly wrong, you can't just deny the issue. Trying to smooth over the problem will work against you, because people know it's not true. Also, when you try to minimize a crisis, you start to bear the responsibility of covering it up. And as we know, the cover up is often worse than the crisis itself. So don't put yourself in a position of pretending like a crisis doesn't exist or saying things that may be perceived as you trying to cover it up, because all of that will hurt you.

The second step is to show action. That means actually doing something about the crisis—making a plan to correct the situation, apologizing to people who have been hurt, and determining options to compensate and make things right for those who have been affected by the problem. Acknowledging the situation, apologizing, and taking steps to right the issue is the best way to get yourself out of a crisis situation and do it well.

That said, once again, you can't simply communicate once that you've made a mistake and plan to fix it. The companies that come out of crises most successfully are the ones that communicate multiple times throughout the crisis itself and the resolution process. They explain what actions they're taking to make the current situation right, and what they're doing to ensure this problem will never surface again.

Knowing When to Step Away

The second rule of crisis communication is that if you get in a fight with a pig, you both get muddy, but the pig likes it. And what that means is when people are trying to engage with you because they think you're terrible and want to excoriate you publicly—you're better off not engaging in that conversation. The conversation is only meant to make you look even worse. What we recommend is that when you are communicating externally and you get a comment that seems like someone might be trying to bait you into a negative, unproductive conversation, have a prepared initial response. This could be something like, "We appreciate your concern, and we'd like to talk with you directly about it," which you respond to publicly on the original comment. This acknowledges their concern if it is legitimate, and it creates an opportunity for further dialogue. And once you have that dialogue, and you have had a one-on-one together, as humans, focusing on building relationships and finding a solution, then in a lot of cases, you can turn the negative situation around.

Now, as the great Taylor Swift once said in her song *Shake it Off*, "haters gonna hate" (Swift 2014). There are some people who will just never be happy until everybody is covered in mud. Especially when people are interacting online and can choose to be anonymous, they don't have to act like their genuine selves or acknowledge the person reading on the other side of the screen. There are people who are going to be angry and upset, and you cannot change their minds because they're deep in this online persona that can rage without dealing with the usual social consequences of interacting face to face. In those situations, you just need to acknowledge that you can't make everybody happy. As long as your highest priority, targeted audiences and the people who you really care about are responding okay, you're going to be okay. That focus and prioritization of audiences will also help you stay focused on what matters through a crisis situation. It'll also help you avoid getting in that fight with a pig (or a troll, to use the more popular term in Internet communities).

We worked with a company where the CEO had almost exactly the same name as a man who was captured on Instagram screaming racist and homophobic slurs at his neighbor. And unfortunately, people thought that this man was our client. Our client started getting lots of messages through their website and on the phone, death threats, and hostile comments that they were concerned were really going to hurt their reputation.

Our approach was to be very open and authentic and prove beyond any doubt that it was not our client who said those terrible things. And we did that by recording and releasing a video to clarify who this client was.

We also let people know what the company's values are. This company had always been focused on family. So we helped them draft a diversity statement that was true to their core company values, which they could use to reinforce their values and position for the rest of their existence. We communicated the statement regularly and we set it as the primary pop-up when you hit their homepage. Most importantly, we followed through on this statement by taking action and coordinating a donation on behalf of our client to a local organization. And over the course of a couple of days, we'd significantly decreased the volume of messages coming to ruin their reputation. So, communicating with video authentically, honestly, and humanely, and reinforcing the company's values through diversity inclusion statements, really helped them get back their reputation and do it quickly.

Another situation with clients that did not go the way it should have was related to an executive director of a nonprofit who was accused of sexual harassment and conduct. Initially, he denied it. It turned out he'd kept a lot of things secret that kept coming to light. There were more and more accusations, and the situation began snowballing. The mistake that he made at that time was not to be completely open and honest about what was going on, so we didn't know the whole story.

We like to say that there are three people you tell everything to and keep no secrets from: your lawyer, your spiritual counsel (whether that's a priest, a pastor, a rabbi, or your mom), and your PR people. Your PR support can't create a communication plan for what they don't know about, and then they cannot help you. You put them in a position where they can't do their best work because they don't have all the critical information. The last thing you want to do is surprise your PR team, because they cannot make sure that they are thinking ahead for you or being proactive for you if you don't tell them everything that they need to know. Even in cases where silence is the best response, handling a crisis effectively should always begin with speaking to the teams who will support you as you find the right solution that fits your situation.

CHAPTER 8

Building a Human-Centered Social Media Team

Think back to that football stadium full of 70,000 of the most important people in the world to your organization. There are your best employees, prospective employees, investors, customers, suppliers, industry leaders, reporters, and others. There is a stage set at the center of the field. On the stage is a microphone that will amplify every word to everyone in the seats. You also have access to the mega screen to share photos and videos so everyone can view them. What do you do? Who do you send to talk with all these incredibly important people?

This is what you should be thinking about as you hire for any social media position. When you interview a social media practitioner, consider whether they would know what to say, how to say it, how to include videos and photos, and how to keep people's attention. If your social media effort is going well, this is exactly what you can expect. The people you choose to manage your social media will have the biggest and most important voice for your company on any given day. These people will be responsible for interacting with other people on your behalf more than anyone else.

Selection

What is the personification of your company brand? No, really. If your company came to life as a human being, what would that person be like? Of course, they would live out your values. Would they be upbeat and positive, or serious and skeptical? Would they use simple language and emojis? Or technical language and acronyms? Would they be the most popular person in the room? Or would they thrive in a small group of highly focused professionals? Your brand representative can come to life as a cheerleader, an athlete, a scientist, a writer, an adventurer, a designer, or any other role you can imagine. Who does your most important audience want and need you to be?

None of this is to say that you need to hire social media people who are all of these things themselves—they just need to understand who your company needs to be in order to interact with humans well. Social media practitioners need to be able to communicate in this style every day in every situation. They need to be able to articulate how your company would promote a product or service very differently from how the competition would—even if the product or service is exactly the same.

So how do you find these people? We came across an article once, years ago, about how the future workforce will be led by people with table-shaped brains. These people had one "leg" able to understand data and analytics, one "leg" that was able to communicate with emotional intelligence, and a "top" that connected the two with strategy. This is the ideal type of brain to engage for social media positions.

Great social media people can be hard to find based on their resumes. The first thing to look for is someone who is a communicator, not necessarily a marketer. Those who have degrees in PR, journalism, or communications tend to be better at understanding and talking with people. Some marketers, on the other hand, will be so focused on *what*— what graphic, what campaign, what post—that they have a harder time taking a human-centric approach to social media. Next, look for resumes where people tout their social media accomplishments with numbers and data. Look for those who include numbers outside of the channels they mention. Yes, it is great to increase a Facebook page from 250 followers to 25,000, but what impact did that have on the business? Finally, look for someone who is able to teach others about social media. Are they part of groups or associations, do they sit on boards, have they hosted training sessions, did they work with executives on their social media accounts? All of these things are indicators of the "table top," or their ability to make strategic connections.

After vetting people through their resumes, take a look at their social media channels (or have HR do this for you). Are they active and interacting with others regularly? Are they connected in the community? Do they take their digital footprint seriously, or is it a joke? If they have very little presence on social media, that's not necessarily cause to worry. Some practitioners choose to keep a low profile personally. Then, look at the social media channels they currently manage. Are there interactions or are they just posting? What personality is being showcased?

In an interview, the most important thing to determine is whether the person communicates easily. Do you like talking with them? Do they ask good questions? Do they seem genuinely interested in you and the company? When you're evaluating their responses to questions, consider whether they seem trustworthy, and whether they can talk about what they do in simple, human terms. Depending on your brand's personification, you may be looking for a social media candidate to incorporate a certain amount of data, details, or stories as they respond to you. Once they get to know your company, this person is going to be the one in front of that stadium of 70,000 of your most important people. If things are going badly at the company, could you trust this person to step up and say the right thing?

Before you hire anyone to work in social media for your company, you need to be sure that they are good communicators. This is often easy to test. Ask them to write a narrative about your company and what makes it special. This simple assignment will identify whether they can research your company and competitors online, write in a way that is compelling, and understand the context in which they will be communicating on your behalf. Don't give them a word count—let them use as many or as few words as they would like, although less is often better than more. Encourage them to include visual aids if they like, and look for people who develop their own graphics or choose ones that are human-centric and emotional. Look for those who use data and provable facts in their narrative, since the best people will think that way.

Training

At our company, we believe that training should support a career map. Working with social media practitioners and building a team works best when each person has a roadmap for where they would like to advance in their career. We find that social media people can advance in a number of ways if given the right support, since they are natural communicators.

Whenever we begin coaching or mentoring a practitioner, we always start at the end. What role would the person like to hold by the point that they're ready to retire? Once we know where someone wants to end up in their career, there are four typical paths most people will take to get there: strategy, management, operations, and business development.

Strategists are big thinkers and visionaries. They see the future of social media marketing, and they are obsessed with where the channels are headed. They keep themselves informed about changes and new developments across different social platforms. They balance that interest in social media with a strong interest in people. Often, they are interested in psychology and sociology. They understand what people want, they are good at listening, and their research skills are excellent. For these people, we focus on external professional development. We encourage them to attend all the conferences they can, give them opportunities to present, and encourage them to write blogs and bylined articles. They are typically amazing individual contributors and work best in partnership with, but not management over, other people. Strategists are often recognized for their creative genius and lead the direction of the marketing group.

Managers are great at leading and developing other people. They want to grow and build a team. Mentoring gets them excited, as does ensuring that others are being recognized for their contributions. They are able to see and understand all the moving parts of what a social media team does: content strategy, channel management, community development, issues management, customer service, event support, advertising, data analysis, and so forth. They know what is needed to execute a strategy, and they will always get it done. For them, we focus on management training and development. We ensure they have all the tools and techniques they need to be great at helping others be successful. They learn how to recruit, train, manage, correct, and terminate their direct reports. These folks usually follow a traditional management path into higher levels of people leadership.

There are people who thrive on process and organization. They always have their work done early so that they can work on refining the processes and methods for how the company's entire social media marketing operation runs. They are obsessed with data and analytics to make sure the social media team is performing at their best. They create new systems, they organize editorial content, and they bring new ideas to the table about how the team can work better together. Project management fulfills them. For these professionals, we look internally and externally for training and development focused on operational excellence. They manage marketing operations and ultimately end up being the ones who make sure everything runs smoothly.

"Compelling" is the only word to describe some social media practitioners. They are amazing at convincing people online to get involved; they rally communities; they calm upset or angry people; and they know how to sell an idea, a contest, a new product, or a new approach to services. While they may come from social media, they often end up in sales or industry relations. They are "out there" all the time, never afraid to be the biggest advocate for the company. When an organization has sales and marketing reporting to one person, these folks often make the move into the sales side of the business. They can also become external spokespeople who hit the road and are out convincing others to buy from, partner with, or invest in the company. They need mentoring from others as well as a chance to present themselves and the strategists' ideas. You will not regret it.

Resiliency

Speaking to 7,000, or 70,000, or 7,000,000 people every day on behalf of a company can be incredibly stressful, even for those who are good at their job and used to it. Social media is a high-pressure job. Everything is public, all your work is on display, and everyone thinks they can do it better. On top of all this, social media practitioners are often the people who get the wrath of angry people and trolls. They are often personally attacked and insulted. Even "low stress" industries can experience interferences and crises that fall on the social media team to explain or alleviate.

During 2020 and 2021, as the COVID pandemic bore down on companies around the world, social media became a primary communication channel even for companies that had little or no social media activity prior to the pandemic. That meant that most of the responsibility for communicating externally—and for some companies, with their own employees—suddenly ended up on the shoulders of practitioners. At the same time, company leaders were isolated from their teams and their social media communities, as they could easily work from home. Bringing marketing people back was the lowest priority for most companies. Crises abounded as employees were laid off or furloughed, supply chains were unable to meet demand, hours changed constantly, and so did local, state, and national regulations. Social media teams could barely keep up, and if they shared anything inaccurate, they were immediately held accountable.

For all these reasons, social media practitioners burn out, often quickly and without warning. They leave for easier, less stressful, and less intense marketing positions. People who manage and run these teams must realize that just like their audiences, their practitioners are also people. Imagine, just for a second, standing on that stage in that stadium while everyone yells at you. What would you need to stay standing, let alone speaking, in the face of daily backlash? Smart marketing leaders put coaching and resiliency consultants in place to support their teams. They give them more time off, practice mental health awareness, and provide opportunities to try different growth paths. They talk regularly with social media practitioners about how they are doing, what excites them, and where they want to go.

While we are not psychologists by any means, we know that resilient team members have a large and active community internally at work and externally in other marketing departments. Nothing is more powerful than people.

CHAPTER 9

Measuring for Improvement

Many social media practitioners focus on brand impressions, reach, and frequency in their reports, and this data-driven analysis is shared with others in their company. While all those metrics are important, the most important thing that a social media practitioner can do today is to inform the company about people. So many people in leadership positions for companies can end up removed from people who have the biggest day-to-day impact on the business—and that presents challenges. It can be harder to build meaningful relationships and understand what key audiences really care about. But social media practitioners are uniquely positioned within companies to know that well, if they're taking advantage of opportunities to listen and make people a priority.

We talked earlier in the book about how all social media channels should have job descriptions. As you are measuring and reporting on those channels, don't focus too hard on how many impressions each channel generates, but on how well they have done their jobs. Every month should be a job performance review for those channels. We should understand how well they did in getting us closer to people. We should be able to tell others the value of conversations and relationships that we've created. If the social media team communicates this well, there will no longer be a question about whether or not to invest in social media. Social media will become one of the most critical functions of the entire business.

Ultimately, our social media impact on people is what we most want to understand, and what we should be measuring. How many relationships have we created and strengthened? What opportunities do those people present to the company? How many unhappy people have we neutralized or created positive relationships with? Understanding how many actual human beings we've reached and actual interactions we've shared will tell us the most about what social media means for our company. In the same vein, your next step isn't just about hitting a follower count metric or measuring the next set of impressions. Think about how to get closer to the people you care about, how to get them more deeply involved with the company and supportive of your success. We as social media practitioners have that responsibility. And if we think about social media as people first, all of this will come naturally.

Glossary

1. *Feed*—A feed on social media is a generic term for the stream of content you see from other users. On most social networks, the feed functions as a homepage and is the most common way to see people's posts and engage with them.
2. *Follower*—A follower is a user on social media who has subscribed to see your posts in their feed. Both personal and business accounts can have followers. Your number of followers, or follower count, is a key metric for seeing how your audience on social media is growing or shrinking over time.
3. *Engagement rate*—A social media metric that tells you how much a post is motivating people to interact with it. It's defined as (number of people who engaged with your post divided by the number of people who saw your post) × 100 percent. Typically, a higher engagement rate means your post was more compelling (or at least more likely to provoke a response). Engagement rate is difficult to compare across social networks, as what counts as an "engagement" and what counts as "seeing your post" is different on each network. "Seeing your post" could refer to reach or impressions, while "engagements" may include likes, comments, shares, reactions, and more.
4. *Impressions*—A social media metric that measures how many times your post has been shown in users' feeds. Unlike with reach, you may count multiple impressions for a single user if they have looked at your post more than once. Each social network counts impressions differently—on Facebook and Instagram a post.
5. *Viral*—Viral is a term describing content that spreads exponentially on social media. This typically occurs because an increasing number of people share the content with their followers, then their followers share the same content to their followers and so on, creating a snowball effect. Creating content that goes viral is the holy grail of social media marketing, as it means you get a huge audience without spending a cent (Gollin 2021).

References

Cahn, N. 2020. "Tips for Women—And Men—Who Want to be Influencers." *Forbes*, January 16, 2020. https://www.forbes.com/sites/naomicahn/2020/01/16/tips-for-women—and-men—who-want-to-be-influencers/?sh=217614f84164.

Geyser, W. August 18, 2021. "The State of Influencer Marketing 2021: Benchmark Report." *Influencer Marketing Hub*. https://influencermarketinghub.com/influencer-marketing-benchmark-report-2021/.

Geyser, W. 2022. "TikTok Statistics–63 TikTok Stats You Need to Know [2022 Update]." *Influencer Marketing Hub*, March 31, 2022. https://influencer-marketinghub.com/tiktok-stats/.

Gollin, M. January 10, 2020. "The 65 Social Media Terms & Definitions to Know in 2021." *Falcon.io*. www.falcon.io/insights-hub/topics/social-media-management/social-media-terms-buzzwords-definitions-marketers-need-to-know/.

LinkedIn Talent Solutions. 2015. "The Ultimate List of Hiring Statistics for Hiring Managers, HR Professionals, and Recruiters." *Global Talent Trends*. https://business.linkedin.com/content/dam/business/talent-solutions/global/en_us/c/pdfs/Ultimate-List-of-Hiring-Stats-v02.04.pdf.

Magretta, J. 2011. *Understanding Michael Porter*. Brighton, Massachusetts: Harvard Business Review Press.

Newberry, C. January 06, 2021. "44 Instagram Stats That Matter to Marketers in 2021." *Hootsuite*. https://blog.hootsuite.com/instagram-statistics/.

Nguyen, J. and Hallett, K. May 23, 2021. "How to Use the Emotion Wheel to Better Understand Your Feelings." *Mind Body Green*. https://www.mindbodygreen.com/articles/emotion-wheel/.

Pew Research Center. April 07, 2021. "Social Media Fact Sheet." *Pew Research Center*. www.pewresearch.org/internet/fact-sheet/social-media/.

Statista Research Department. September 07, 2021. "Distribution of Pinterest Users Worldwide as of July 2021, by Gender." *Statista*. www.statista.com/statistics/248168/gender-distribution-of-pinterest-users/.

Swift, T. 2014. "Shake It Off." *Big Machine Records*. https://spotify.com/album/2Z51EnLF4Nps4LmulSQPnn (accessed September 14, 2021).

Taylor, K. May 09, 2019. "Kim Kardashian Revealed in a Lawsuit That She Demands up to Half a Million Dollars for a Single Instagram Post and Other details About How Much She Charges for Endorsement Deals." *Business Insider*. www.businessinsider.com/how-much-kim-kardashian-charges-for-instagram-endorsement-deals-2019-5.

Resources

Slice Communications, LLC

Slice Communications, LLC exists to get people to pay attention to our clients. As a leading Philadelphia marketing and communications agency, it is who we are as people, what gets us up in the morning, and what keeps us going. Since our founding, we have put our collective innate need for attention to work for our clients. We are proud that we have helped them achieve their business goals and grow strategically. Visit us at www.slicecommunications.com to find out the ways in which we can help you achieve your marketing and communications goals.

Additional Publications

Additional publications by Cass Bailey and Dana Schmidt include:

- *How to Create and Promote Thought Leadership Content Every Week*;
- *Employer Brand Communications*;
- *Marketing Planning Simplified*;
- *Engagement Marketing*;
- *An Executive's Guide to Confidence in Marketing*; and
- *7 Ways PR Can Grow Your Business*.

Check out all of these publications and more at slicecommunications.com/our-publications.

Social Media Day PHL

Cass and Dana are both proud Board Directors of Social Media Day PHL. An official 501(c)(3) nonprofit since 2020, Social Media Day PHL provides professional development and networking experiences to members of the social media, marketing, and communications community. In addition, SMD hosts an annual #SMDayPHL conference which is the most prominent gathering of communications professionals in the Philadelphia area to hear from top industry experts. Learn more at smdayphl.com.

About the Authors

Cassandra (Cass) M. Bailey is the CEO of Slice Communications, the founder of Social Media Day, Inc., which hosts an annual conference and provides programming for digital communications professionals on the East Coast, and the creator of the "My Mom Is..." book series. She has been working in marketing communications for more than 20 years. She believes that integrated public relations, social media, and e-mail marketing efforts are critical for growing businesses looking to accomplish their business goals.

Cass brings a wide variety of experiences to the communications strategies she develops for the firm's clients. With a background in international politics, economics, and philosophy, communications has become her passion and she has been tapped by various industry associations and the media to share her insights and experiences in the field with appearances on *Good Morning America*, *CBS This Morning*, and *The Today Show*. Cass has also been named as a *WBENC Rising Star* and received the *Brava* award from *Philadelphia TopCEO*.

Cass is deeply involved with her community, serving as Marketing Communications Chair for both the Entrepreneurs Organization of Philadelphia and the Business Leadership Forum at The Union League of Philadelphia; Executive Committee Member of the Small Business Board at the Greater Philadelphia Chamber of Commerce; Chair Emerita of the Board for Tree House Books; and Secretary Emerita of the Board for Hopeworks 'N Camden. Cass graduated from The Catholic University of America with a degree in international politics, economics, and philosophy.

Dana M. Schmidt is the Chief Strategy Officer at Slice Communications. Driven by her passion for digital marketing, Dana champions brand storytelling across social media, PR and e-mail platforms.

Dana's work has taken her from her hometown in Bucks County to New York City, to Denver, and back to Philadelphia—and even earned her an Emmy award along the way for her work on the "Women and Girls Lead" series at Rocky Mountain PBS. She has shared her expertise with digital marketers through outlets like *Adweek*, *NBC10*, *Actions News Inside Story* and as a speaker at several national conferences, such as Social Media Day Inc. Prior to joining the Slice team, Dana worked as the Director of Social Media for Visit Philly.

Having earned her Bachelor's degree in Communications from New York University, Dana returned to NYU for her Master of Fine Arts in Creative Writing. Although she'd like to start her novel in her free time, she is more likely out hiking with her husband, Jesse, their son, Cooper, daughter, Mia, and their husky, Ghost.

Index

active listening, 49, 50, 54
applicant survey, 26
aspirational competitors, 39–40
awards and recognition, 26–27

business-to-business (B2B), 8, 9
business-to-consumer (B2C), 8–9

centers of influence, 29–31
champion readiness review, 27
clarity, 30
comarketing dollars, 35
communications
    with employees, 80–81
    managing, 84
    one-to-one, 34
    with partners, 81–82
    with the public, 82–84
    situations, 84–86
community, 31
competitors, 37–40, 56–57
consistency, 31
content review, 28
conversation openers, 50–51
COVID-19 pandemic, 9, 19, 36
customers and clients, 22–24,
    42–43

data analysis, 55–56
demographics, 19–22, 46
direct competitors, 38
diversity and inclusion commitment,
    27
donors, 33–35

Emotion Wheel (Plutchik), 28–29
employees, 24–29
    communication with, 80–81
    survey, 25–26
engagement rate, 71, 73

Facebook, 6–10, 13–15, 55
feed, 2, 3, 10, 28, 43, 65, 70, 72, 82
follower, 8, 34, 41, 42, 44, 46, 47, 56,
    69–71, 73, 74, 76, 77, 88, 93

human-centric approach
    resiliency, 91–92
    selection, 87–89
    training, 89–91
human resources (HR), 25

impressions, 8, 11, 12, 24, 70–72, 93, 94
indirect competitors, 38–39
influencers, 56
    marketing, 69–70
    measuring impact, 76–78
    program, 72–76
    types of, 70–72
Instagram, 12–13, 71, 72, 74, 76–78
Intel, 35
interceptions, 52–53
investors, 31–34, 44

job description audit, 27

LinkedIn, 9–10, 23, 26, 28, 33, 60,
    61, 65, 73

March Madness, 24
marketing, 19
    campaign, 29, 35–37, 43
    communications, 21, 38
    HR and, 25
    influencer, 69–70, 78
    planning, 21, 22, 32, 33, 35
    strategy, 8, 21–23, 38–40
    top-of-mind, 29–30
mission, vision, and values worksheet, 26

online reputation audit, 26

partners, 35, 44
  communication with, 81–82
  competitors, 39
passive listening, 49, 54, 55, 57
perceived competitors, 39
Pfizer, 36
Pinterest, 13–14
psychographics, 19–22, 46

resiliency, 91–92

simplicity, 29–30
social media
  channels, 6, 13, 14, 16, 23, 28, 43,
    45, 47, 49, 50, 55, 63, 72, 81,
    88, 89, 93

improvements, 93–94
job description, 17
practitioners, 54–56, 63, 87–89,
    91–94
  team, 23, 54, 62, 63, 65, 79,
    90–93
suppliers, 35–37
surveys, 53–54

TikTok, 13, 15–16, 73
Twitter, 10–11

voice and tone, 64–67

YouTube, 14–15

OTHER TITLES IN THE BUSINESS CAREER DEVELOPMENT COLLECTION

Vilma Barr, Consultant, Editor

- *Pay Attention!* by Cassandra Bailey and Dana M. Schmidt
- *Burn Ladders. Build Bridges.* by Alan M. Patterson
- *Decoding Your STEM Career* by Peter Devenyi
- *A Networking Playbook* by Darryl Howes
- *The Street-Smart Side of Business* by Tara Acosta
- *Rules Don't Work for Me* by Gail Summers
- *Fast Forward Your Career* by Simonetta Lureti and Lucio Furlani
- *Shaping Your Future* by Rita Rocker
- *Emotional Intelligence at Work* by Richard M. Contino and Penelope J. Holt
- *How to Use Marketing Techniques to Get a Great Job* by Edward Barr
- *Negotiate Your Way to Success* by Kasia Jagodzinska
- *How to Make Good Business Decisions* by J.C. Baker
- *Ask the Right Questions; Get the Right Job* by Edward Barr
- *Personal and Career Development* by Claudio A. Rivera and Elza Priede
- *Your GPS to Employment Success* by Beverly A. Williams
- *100 Skills of the Successful Sales Professional* by Alex Dripchak
- *Getting It Right When It Matters Most* by Tony Gambill and Scott Carbonara

Concise and Applied Business Books

The Collection listed above is one of 30 business subject collections that Business Expert Press has grown to make BEP a premiere publisher of print and digital books. Our concise and applied books are for...

- Professionals and Practitioners
- Faculty who adopt our books for courses
- Librarians who know that BEP's Digital Libraries are a unique way to offer students ebooks to download, not restricted with any digital rights management
- Executive Training Course Leaders
- Business Seminar Organizers

Business Expert Press books are for anyone who needs to dig deeper on business ideas, goals, and solutions to everyday problems. Whether one print book, one ebook, or buying a digital library of 110 ebooks, we remain the affordable and smart way to be business smart. For more information, please visit www.businessexpertpress.com, or contact sales@businessexpertpress.com.

CPSIA information can be obtained
at www.ICGtesting.com
Printed in the USA
BVHW091001110722
641515BV00006B/19

9 781637 422625